Vulnerable to Grace

Vulnerable to Grace

to

Grace

By
Danny A. Belrose

'You are called
to create pathways
in the world for peace'

A Study and Worship Resource Exploring Section 163

Printed in the United States of America

13 12 11 10 09 08   5 4 3 2 1

ISBN: 978-0-8309-1416-6

Watercolor cover art by Danny Belrose

Acknowledgments

How do I get through,

    using these frail, fragile containers, God,

    these letters woven into words

    short-changed of meaning?

Tired, over-worked, always wanting,

    they carry that which cannot be carried:

    the joy and hurt of the heart's song

    that sleepy letters cannot sing.

My hopes, dreams, and deepest feelings escape utterance

    because the clothes don't fit.

They wrap themselves in hidden beauty.

Peeking, seeking, teasing, like a childhood game,

    their meaning unannounced by sayings, sounds,

    and soft winds of scattered thoughts.

So much unclaimed, unheard, unrealized.

Prayer without wings. Breath without air.

And yet, despite my wordless cries

    You are deep inside and hear me.

                    —D.A. Belrose

The challenge and struggle to wrap thoughts and feelings into words that "get through" is every author's bane and is never a solitary task. Many people have unknowingly contributed to this work through conversations shared, sermons heard, lessons taught, films seen, and books read. Others have graciously reviewed the manuscript and provided helpful insights. I am particularly indebted to David R. Brock, Peter A. Judd, Jane M. Gardner, and Cheryll L. Peterman, whose editing skills and creative suggestions were invaluable.

Contents

Preface

I speak through the prophets to give clear pictures of the way things are. Using prophets, I tell revealing stories....Are you going to repeat the life of your ancestor Jacob?....Your real identity is formed through God-sent prophets, who led you out of Egypt and served as faithful pastors.

—Excerpts from Hosea 12:10–13 The Message[1]

The 2007 World Conference was much different from previous conferences. Our call to be a prophetic people found its voice in a program that encouraged all delegates to participate in "discernment groups," where through guided reflection, scripture, and silence we sought to more fully discern what matters most for the Community of Christ at a time when many issues vie for our energy and attention.

Discernment, of course, is an on-going process as witnessed by our continual desire to discover "clear pictures of the way things are" and should be. Prophecy is not exclusively future oriented or predictive—it is inspired utterance of divine truth arising from the past, existing in the present, and calling us to God's future.

The Conference approved for inclusion in the Doctrine and Covenants "Words of Counsel to the Church," presented by President Stephen M. Veazey. The format for my exploration of what has now become Doctrine and Covenants Section 163 will include reflections on each of the document's paragraphs, questions for discussion, worship helps and hymn texts, and concluding comments on the document as a whole. Before proceeding with that task, let me offer some reflections regarding canonization of scripture.

Brother Veazey's testimony of Section 163 (pages 11 to 13) is a candid and poignant profile of his experience and personal epiphany in receiving and processing the words of counsel:

> I began to sense some emerging direction that I needed to bring to the church. I am not sure how to describe this, except to say that I felt a drawing power that focused my thinking on certain themes. I had a persistent awareness of truth seeking expression in words. I wrestled in my mind and with my dictionary to find words worthy of the truth I had met.

When President Veazey presented the words of counsel to the World Conference he had not made a determination as to their official status. Striving to be open to the Spirit's guiding, President Veazey put the matter in the hands of the church. This speaks not only to his humility but to his willingness to trust the church and to also trust the words of counsel to stand on their own merit—to reveal their own source. This is not the first time that inspired counsel has been placed before us without specific instruction regarding its disposition. President Grant McMurray shared portions of what was to become Section 161 four years before they were included in the Doctrine and Covenants:

> On April 21, 1996, I brought to the church words of counsel which I felt led to share, without any specific instruction as to their ultimate disposition. I felt it was important that the church live with the words and not feel compelled to make any urgent decisions about them. (Preface to Section 161)

Meaning no disrespect for the actions of the World Conference to lobby for and approve Section 163 as scripture, I believe the willingness "to allow the church to live with the words" of inspired counsel has wisdom. This may become increasingly important, as World Conferences will be convened every three years rather than biennially. Traditionally we have knit the receiving and approving of inspired counsel together to the point that they have been become in essence, synonymous. Albeit unintentional, this practice can disenfranchise non-English-speaking delegates from full participation in the canonization process when sufficient time for accurate translations is not provided. Perhaps we can look to a day when words of counsel (in several languages) will be published in the *Herald* and posted on the church's Web site months or even years before their canonization.

Inspired counsel, or what we popularly refer to as "revelation," is a foundational tenet of our faith. Despite how clearly such guidance is articulated, it is forever wanting. There is always slippage between what is intended and what is expressed. To quote Peter Judd, former member of the First Presidency, "The divine-human experience of revelation is one thing and that which we have on the printed page is another." Joseph Campbell, perhaps the world's foremost authority on mythology, talked about the divine-human experience in this way:

> God is a thought. God is a name. God is an idea. But its reference is to something that transcends all

---

[1.] Eugene H. Peterson's *The Message* is a contemporary rendering of the Bible from the original languages, crafted to present its tone, rhythm, events, and ideas in everyday language.

[2] Joseph Campell, *Joseph Campbell: The Power of Myth with Bill Moyers*, Betty Sue Fowlers, ed. (New York: Doubleday, 1988), 49.

thinking. The ultimate mystery of being is beyond all categories of thought….The best things can't be told because they transcend thought. The second best are misunderstood, because those are the thoughts that are supposed to refer to that which can't be thought about. The third best are what we talk about.[2]

President Veazey's testimony candidly confirms the difficulties experienced in adequately capturing divine insight with words.

> I also continued to wrestle with the Words of Counsel, never satisfied that what I wrote was enough to express the divine will. In God's presence, we become acutely aware of the limits of our human abilities, including our language. The experience is deeply humbling. (See "Doctrine Covenants 163: My Testimony" by Stephen M. Veazey, page 11 of this work)

The question is, how do we discern the validity of inspired utterance? How do we ascertain that couched within the frail words of human communication the mind and will of God is being expressed? One way is to examine previous canonical writings, comparing what has been said before with what is being said now. Is there harmony or dichotomy—is there a sense of consistency and congruence?

Consistency is an important test, yet its focus is primarily "content"—on *what* is being said and *how,* as opposed to *by* whom and *to* whom. In a sense, it places limitations on God and on us. In the extreme, it reduces the revelatory experience to redundancy. What if the Spirit desires to tell us something new, something radically disjunctive? Ironically, revelation is disjunctive by nature—it uncovers what was unknown or hidden. Revelation does not require precedent but rather creates precedent. The primary test of revelation is the gift of discernment.

I have been married for forty-seven years to my wife, Penelope. Although I can usually predict how she will respond in a given situation, there are times when she will offer an opinion and I will say with astonishment, "I didn't know you believed that!" I am suddenly privy to information that is revelatory—it doesn't fit with anything she has said before. However, despite the fact that this information is new, possibly even disconcerting, I *always recognize* her voice. I recognize her voice because we have spent a lifetime together in a day-to-day, loving, intimate relationship. What the Spirit reveals to us, through the words of prophetic servants, may be surprising, disjunctive, and unsettling. But when we have a day-to-day relationship with the Source of this guidance, there will be no mistaking the Spirit's voice.

The church's love affair with revelation has seen us at times more enamored with the idea of divine disclosure than what is being said. I have seen people rush out of a worship service ecstatic because an inspired message was given only to hear someone say, "I don't remember exactly what was said, but you should have been there. It was wonderful!" On the other hand, we sometimes reduce revelation to information. We seem to want to add more and more to the canon of contemporary scripture when we make meager use of what is presently there.

That having been said, words *do* change us. Inspired utterance can awaken and transform us. The language of the soul infused by the language of the Spirit breathes an epiphany, and epiphanies (canonized or not canonized) are life-changing. Anne Lamott beautifully describes a personal awakening while reading *The Only Dance There Is* by Ram Dass:

> This was the day I pecked a hole out of the cocoon and saw the sky of ingredients that would constitute my spiritual path. This was the day I knew the ingredients of the spiritual that would serve me—love, poetry, meditation, community. I knew that sex could be as sacred as taking care of the poor. I knew that no one comes holier than anyone else, that nowhere is better than anywhere else. I knew that the resurrection of the mind was possible. I knew that no matter how absurd and ironic it was, acknowledging death and the finite was what gave you life and presence. You might as well make it good. Nature, family, children, cadavers, births, rivers in which we pee and bathe, splash and flirt and float memorial candles—in those you would find holiness.[3]

As with all scripture, Section 163 will bless the church as we continue to discern its deeper meanings and message. In and through its words we will find holiness that spills out into the everydayness of our lives, calling us individually and as a faith community to be whom God is urging us to be. There is far more to be mined from the text of Section 163 than any solitary voice can or will discern. My reflections then are cursory and merely scratch the surface of inspired counsel that calls us to "be vulnerable to divine grace."

From the many memorable phrases in Section 163 I selected the title *Vulnerable to Grace* for this study, not simply because these two terms, poetically fused together, are powerful, but because, perhaps at no other time does the dance between vulnerability and grace speak to this generation—a generation that desperately needs epiphanies and guidance.

We never outgrow our need for inspired utterance.

---

[3] Anne Lamott, *Grace (Eventually): Thoughts on Faith* (New York: Riverhead Books, 2007), 10–11.

The Divine-human experience pecks "a hole out of the cocoon" and presents us with a "sky of ingredients" that can constitute our spiritual path. To paraphrase Hosea's words, it grants us "a clearer picture of the way things are" so we no longer need to repeat the inadequacies of the past. Revelation must be more than ecstasy and information; it must be transformational. Revelation is never complete until there is a change in attitude and behavior. The focus of Jesus' ministry was neither to educate nor entertain us, but to change us.

Doctrine and Covenants 163: My Testimony

By Stephen M. Veazey

Many months before the 2007 World Conference, I began prayerfully focusing on the needs and opportunities before the church. As I traveled throughout the church, I listened carefully to the concerns and hopes of many. A few topics were prevalent: church identity, priesthood accountability, the nature of scripture, and the connection between belief in Christ and the call to engage in justice and peacemaking.

During a retreat with ethnic ministers, statements of personal pain about the prevalence of racism and sexism in the church moved me deeply. Despite our words about "community in Christ" and the "worth of all persons," it became obvious that our behaviors and our vision are not in full alignment.

As the time for Conference approached, I scheduled time away from the busyness of the office to ground myself in prayer, meditation, and scripture study. I began to respond to a growing spiritual hunger to read prophetic writings from the scriptures. I focused on some of the Old Testament prophets who were strong voices for immigrants, the poor, and those people relegated to the fringes of society.

I began to sense some emerging direction that I needed to bring to the church. I am not sure how to describe this, except to say that I felt a drawing power that focused my thinking on certain themes. I had a persistent awareness of truth seeking expression in words. I wrestled in my mind and with my dictionary to find words worthy of the truth I had met.

During a First Presidency retreat in January 2007, I asked my counselors to review an early draft of the "Words of Counsel." I believe it is important to be accountable to others in matters of the Spirit. We easily assume our thoughts are God's thoughts because of our self-centered tendencies.

After reading the words, my colleagues shared helpful insights in response to my questions and concerns. They encouraged me to stay open to the Spirit and to take the time needed to continue to refine what I was sensing. The months before World Conference were busy as the attention of the Presidency was increasingly on the details of Conference and the proposed legislation that was coming in to International Headquarters. Because of the press of organizational tasks, I had to be intentional about finding time for continued prayer and meditation.

I also continued to wrestle with the Words of Counsel, never satisfied that what I wrote was enough to express the divine will. In God's presence, we become acutely aware of the limits of our human abilities, including our language. The experience is deeply humbling.

There came a point before World Conference when I knew I was going to share the Words of Counsel, but I was not content with what I had prepared. I recall sitting in my study at home. After prayer, I reached for the *Hymns of the Saints* and turned to the section of hymns on revelation. I read beautiful expressions describing the church's yearning and openness for "yet more light and truth." Something surged in me and almost took my breath away. I experienced God's Spirit moving through an intense focus of consciousness and understanding.

I looked at the document again and experienced both a confirmation of direction and need for further refinement. I strove for greater clarity. Some particular phrases came to mind that I had not used before in teaching and preaching. For example, in the closing paragraphs, I endeavored to express the essence of God's love for us and the blessings that would come if we responded. As I did, the phrase "be vulnerable to divine grace" (paragraph 10b) came with great power.

I finished the text for the Words of Counsel the week before World Conference, during the time the International Leaders Meeting (ILM) was occurring. I had opportunity at ILM to teach ideas of peace found in the Doctrine and Covenants. Because some of the participants were new members, I decided to begin by talking about the nature of revelation as expressed in the Doctrine and Covenants. As I was speaking, I experienced confirmation once again of the possible impact for good of the Words of Counsel.

I approached the Sunday night service at World Conference with an unusual mixture of calm and sense of responsibility. That afternoon, I had an opportunity to chat with David Schaal, one of my counselors in the Presidency. I asked him if the Words of Counsel were worthy of that title. He shared a testimony of affirmation with particular spiritual insight that freed me from any further hesitancy.

I will never forget approaching the podium on Sunday evening and looking out over the multitude of faces in the conference chamber. I felt an overwhelming love for our faith community and prayed the words of the message would bring forth good fruit.

As I began speaking, I felt much peace and resolution. The conference chamber was unusually silent; the people spiritually prepared to hear.

As pointed out in the preface to Section 163, I had not made a determination then about what the eventual official status of the counsel would be. I was striving to be open to the Spirit's guiding as it might lead during the Conference and beyond. I sincerely wanted to put the matter in the hands of the church.

Following the evening service, I became aware of a growing possibility that significant groups of people at the Conference would want to consider the document formally for inclusion in the Doctrine and Covenants. However, I decided not to rush a decision, but to remain open to what might happen.

By Monday afternoon, I began to receive correspondence, messages, and e-mails from people at Conference and in other settings. Something was stirring and taking on a life of its own. Messages from some young adults suggested the counsel had given them hope for the church's future and a clearer sense of direction.

These types of responses continued into Tuesday. I read the letters, listened to comments, and continued to pray. I received a moving letter from the Youth Caucus, which included these words: "The bold challenges of earthly stewardship, peace and justice ministries, and priesthood responsibilities left their imprints in our hearts."

I received similar letters from other caucuses, mass meetings, and quorums, including the Council of Twelve. Each letter in its own way expressed the sentiment that the Conference should have the opportunity to consider the Words of Counsel for inclusion in the Doctrine and Covenants. Other letters came that stated affirmation of the Words of Counsel with anticipation that the church would engage in a time of discernment and implementation for some time into the future.

On Wednesday, I met with the Council of Twelve to sustain the council officers, after which we discussed their letter. We explored the issue of not canonizing words of counsel too quickly, so the church could spend time probing the meaning of the words. Surprisingly, even those most concerned about prompt formal action suggested that, in this case, we should go ahead.

Wednesday afternoon I had a long talk with my counselors. We explored various choices and probable implications. I recalled the words of President Robinson, spoken many months before, that I should "remain open" to what could happen at Conference.

I went home and retired to my study, where I sat in silence and prayed for guidance. I reviewed the letters and comments I had received. I began to sense the Words of Counsel were already working in the life of the church and would continue to bear good fruit into the future.

When I thought about releasing the document for formal consideration, I felt a peace at the center of my soul. However, when I thought about waiting, I had an unsettled, even anxious feeling. I made a tentative decision to announce the following morning that I was releasing the document for formal consideration and action. I slept peacefully for the first time in several nights.

The next morning I told Dave Schaal and Becky Savage, my counselors, that I had decided to go ahead with formal consideration and had prepared an announcement to that effect. They gave their full support.

Thursday afternoon and Friday morning, several quorums asked me to meet with them to share my thinking. I expected this, because I knew there was sentiment in the Conference to affirm the document as inspired. I also knew there was the wish to take more time to allow the church-at-large to engage in discernment about its eventual standing. My difficulty was that I agreed with the latter viewpoint based on principle and reason. However, I could not deny the Spirit prompting me to go ahead. I simply decided to share my testimony with the quorums and answer any questions as best I could.

I also decided to share my testimony about my decision with the entire assembly. I tried to make it clear that this course of action was not a reversal of a previous decision, but the result of spiritual discernment in the faith community that had advanced in an unexpected but undeniable way.

The eventual action of the World Conference to approve the Words of Counsel for inclusion in the Doctrine and Covenants was not the conclusion. Rather it was the beginning of serious, churchwide discernment on the meaning of the ideas contained in it.

We have much to talk about: the purpose of the church, the responsible use of scripture, the nature of priesthood, and the purposes of the Temple. Each person and congregation needs to discover prayerfully how to express the principles outlined in Section 163 in local contexts.

In fact, the counsel itself poses one of the most critical discernment questions before the church: As a prophetic people, "what matters most" with the use of our time, attention, and resources in the days ahead?

I am certain, because of my experience with the birth of Doctrine and Covenants 163, of this: God has some big dreams for the church. How we choose to re-spond to God's vision for us as a prophetic people will make all the difference in the years ahead.[4]

---

[4] Stephen M. Veazey, "Doctrine and Covenants 163: My Testimony," *Herald*, July 2007, 12–14.

13

Doctrine and Covenants Section 163

President Stephen M. Veazey submitted the following counsel to the church and to the World Conference on Sunday, March 25, 2007. Following a period of discernment, the counsel was presented to the quorums, councils, and orders of the church and to the World Conference again on Thursday, March 29, to be considered for inclusion in the Doctrine and Covenants. President Veazey prefaced his "Words of Counsel to the Church" with the following introductory statement:

"Every day since being ordained as prophet-president, I have carried the needs of the church on my heart. Sometimes the weight of concern has seemed almost unbearable. Perhaps this is as it should be, because the heaviness of responsibility has pressed me to seek the mind and will of God as never before. Striving to be open to the guidance of the Spirit, while attempting to lay aside my own preconceived notions, has been a challenging but necessary learning experience. And, as I have sought to perceive God's will for the church through prayer, study, and listening for the Creator's voice in the voices of the faith community, I have been blessed by the Spirit in various, sometimes surprising ways.

"The words and images that follow have been birthed through much struggle, not because of any lack of inspiration, but because of the limitations of the human vessel entrusted with responsibility for articulating divine encounter. Attempting to communicate in words what is ultimately beyond words always leaves one with a sense of incompleteness. Added to this is the challenge of creating phrases that can be translated into the languages of the international church without loss of essential meanings. Fortunately, we have the promise that one of the primary functions of the Holy Spirit is to bear witness of divine truth beyond the confines of language and culture.

"Therefore, it is in deep humility and with heartfelt gratitude to God that I offer the following counsel as a witness of God's eternal purpose and continuing activity in the life of the church. In so doing, I place these words in the church's hand, trusting that the Spirit will enable the faith community to hear the call of God today with increasing clarity."

1. "Community of Christ," your name, given as a divine blessing, is your identity and calling. If you will discern and embrace its full meaning, you will not only discover your future, you will become a blessing to the whole creation. Do not be afraid to go where it beckons you to go.

2 a. Jesus Christ, the embodiment of God's shalom, invites all people to come and receive divine peace in the midst of the difficult questions and struggles of life. Follow Christ in the way that leads to God's peace and discover the blessings of all of the dimensions of salvation.

b. Generously share the invitation, ministries, and sacraments through which people can encounter the Living Christ who heals and reconciles through redemptive relationships in sacred community. The restoring of persons to healthy or righteous relationships with God, others, themselves, and the earth is at the heart of the purpose of your journey as a people of faith.

3 a. You are called to create pathways in the world for peace in Christ to be relationally and culturally incarnate. The hope of Zion is realized when the vision of Christ is embodied in communities of generosity, justice, and peacefulness.

b. Above all else, strive to be faithful to Christ's vision of the peaceable Kingdom of God on earth. Courageously challenge cultural, political, and religious trends that are contrary to the reconciling and restoring purposes of God. Pursue peace.

c. There are subtle, yet powerful, influences in the world, some even claiming to represent Christ, that seek to divide people and nations to accomplish their destructive aims. That which seeks to harden one human heart against another by constructing walls of fear and prejudice is not of God. Be especially alert to these influences, lest they divide you or divert you from the mission to which you are called.

4 a. God, the Eternal Creator, weeps for the poor, displaced, mistreated, and diseased of the world because of their unnecessary suffering. Such conditions are not God's will. Open your ears to hear the pleading of mothers and fathers in all nations who desperately seek a future of hope for their children. Do not turn away from them. For in their welfare resides your welfare.

b. The earth, lovingly created as an environment for life to flourish, shudders in distress because creation's natural and living systems are becoming exhausted from carrying the burden of human greed and conflict. Humankind must awaken from its illusion of independence and unrestrained consumption without lasting consequences.

c. Let the educational and community development endeavors of the church equip people of all ages to carry the ethics of Christ's peace into all arenas of life. Prepare new generations of disciples to bring fresh vision to bear on the perplexing problems of poverty, disease, war, and environmental deterioration. Their contributions will be multiplied if their hearts are focused on God's will for creation.

5 a. The Council of Twelve is urged to enthusiastically embrace its calling as apostles of the peace of Jesus Christ in all of its dimensions. The Twelve are sent into the world to lead the church's mission of restoration through relevant gospel proclamation and the establishment of signal communities of justice and peace that reflect the vision of Christ. As the apostles move out in faith and unity of purpose, freeing themselves from other duties, they will be blessed with an increased capacity for sharing Christ's message of hope and restoration for creation.

b. To accelerate the work of sharing the gospel, the Twelve and the Seventy should be closely associated in implementing wholistic evangelistic ministries. The seventy are to be the forerunners of Christ's peace, preparing the way for apostolic witness to be more readily received.

c. Procedures regarding the calling and assignments of the Presidents of Seventy and members of the Quorums of Seventy shall be developed to facilitate the maximum level of collaboration with the Council of Twelve. The Twelve, the Presidents of Seventy, and the Quorums of Seventy should spend sufficient time together to ensure a mutual understanding of evangelistic priorities and approaches.

6 a. Priesthood is a sacred covenant involving the highest form of stewardship of body, mind, spirit, and relationships. The priesthood shall be composed of people of humility and integrity who are willing to extend themselves in service for others and for the well-being of the faith community.

b. Truly authoritative priesthood ministry emerges from a growing capacity to bring blessing to others. Unfortunately, there are some who have chosen to view priesthood as a right of privilege or as a platform for promoting personal perspectives. Others hold priesthood as a casual aspect of their lives without regard to appropriate levels of preparation and response.

c. The expectation for priesthood to continually magnify their callings through spiritual growth, study, exemplary generosity, ethical choices, and fully accountable ministry is always present. How can the Spirit fill vessels that are unwilling to expand their capacity to receive and give according to a full measure of God's grace and truth?

d. Counsel given previously regarding the need to develop ways whereby priesthood can magnify their ministry or determine their commitment to active service remains applicable and should be more intentionally implemented. The First Presidency will provide guidelines for processes to be applied in culturally respectful ways in the various fields of the church. Fundamentally, however, the ultimate responsibility for priesthood faithfulness rests on the individual in response to the needs and expectations of the faith community.

7 a. Scripture is an indispensable witness to the Eternal Source of light and truth, which cannot be fully contained in any finite vessel or language. Scripture has been written and shaped by human authors through experiences of revelation and ongoing inspiration of the Holy Spirit in the midst of time and culture.

b. Scripture is not to be worshiped or idolized. Only God, the Eternal One of whom scripture testifies, is worthy of worship. God's nature, as revealed in Jesus Christ and affirmed by the Holy Spirit, provides the ultimate standard by which any portion of scripture should be interpreted and applied.

c. It is not pleasing to God when any passage of scripture is used to diminish or oppress races, genders, or classes of human beings. Much physical and emotional violence has been done to some of God's beloved children through the misuse of scripture. The church is called to confess and repent of such attitudes and practices.

d. Scripture, prophetic guidance, knowledge, and discernment in the faith community must walk hand in hand to reveal the true will of God. Follow this pathway, which is the way of the Living Christ, and you will discover more than sufficient light for the journey ahead.

8 a. The Temple is an instrument of ongoing revelation in the life of the church. Its symbolism and ministries call people to reverence in the presence of the Divine Being. Transformative encounters with the Eternal Creator and Reconciler await those who follow its spiritual pathways of healing, reconciliation, peace, strengthening of faith, and knowledge.

b. There are additional sacred ministries that will spring forth from the Temple as rivers of living water to help people soothe and resolve the brokenness and pain in their lives. Let the Temple continue to come to life as a sacred center of worship, education, community building, and discipleship preparation for all ages.

c. As these ministries come to fuller expression, receptive congregations in the areas around the Temple and throughout the world will be revived and equipped for more effective ministry. Vital to this awakening is the understanding that the Temple calls the entire church to become a sanctuary of Christ's peace, where people from all nations, ethnicities, and life circumstances can be gathered into a spiritual home without dividing walls, as a fulfillment of the vision for which Jesus Christ sacrificed his life.

9. Faithful disciples respond to an increasing awareness of the abundant generosity of God by sharing according to the desires of their hearts; not by commandment or constraint. Break free of the shackles of conventional culture that mainly promote self-serving interests. Give generously according to your true capacity. Eternal joy and peace await those who grow in the grace of generosity that flows from compassionate hearts without thought of return. Could it be otherwise in the domain of God, who eternally gives all for the sake of creation?

10 a. Collectively and individually, you are loved with an everlasting love that delights in each faithful step taken. God yearns to draw you close so that wounds may be healed, emptiness filled, and hope strengthened.

b. Do not turn away in pride, fear, or guilt from the One who seeks only the best for you and your loved ones. Come before your Eternal Creator with open minds and hearts and discover the blessings of the gospel anew. Be vulnerable to divine grace.

11 a. God is calling for a prophetic community to emerge, drawn from the nations of the world, that is characterized by uncommon devotion to the compassion and peace of God revealed in Jesus Christ. Through divine grace and wisdom, this faith community has been given abundant gifts, resources, and opportunities to equip it to become such a people. Chief among these is the power of community in Christ expressed locally in distinctive fashions while upholding a unity of vision, foundational beliefs, and mission throughout the world.

b. There are many issues that could easily consume the time and energy of the church. However, the challenge before a prophetic people is to discern and pursue what matters most for the journey ahead.

In addition to the words offered above, I want to express my heartfelt love for the church as it is and as it is becoming. Despite the challenges involved, it is my pleasure to be able to serve you, my brothers and sisters in Christ, who have been claimed by the adventurous vision and spirit of the Restoration movement. May we journey into the future trusting one another, confident that the One who called the church into being continues to guide it toward fulfillment of divine purpose.

Grace and Peace,
Stephen M. Veazey
President of the Church
Independence, Missouri
March 29, 2007

Paragraph 1:
Identity and Calling

1. "Community of Christ," your name, given as a divine blessing, is your identity and calling. If you will discern and embrace its full meaning, you will not only discover your future, you will become a blessing to the whole creation. Do not be afraid to go where it beckons you to go.

" 'Community of Christ,' " your name, given as a divine blessing, is your identity and calling."

Recently I was asked, "As a committed Christian, what holds you to the Community of Christ?" My response was as surprising to me as it was to the inquirer. I have been asked this question numerous times over the years and given varied answers, some lengthy, some brief, but rarely as brief as one word. "*Exploration!*" I replied.

It was an answer that needed unpacking, and further conversation touched on the following: "We have always been a people probing and pursuing God's will and way. It has been, and will continue to be, a quest in which we seek not so much to possess Truth as to be possessed by it—to rejoice in it, to weep in it, to turn toward it, more often than not at the expense of our own will. It may sound very self-centered, but I am a member of the Community of Christ because it is the one journey where I will discover who I am and who I am called to be."

God continually calls us to discover who we are in our response to God's highest hopes for creation. The name "Community of Christ" is both our identity and our calling.

"If you will discern and embrace its full meaning, you will not only discover your future, you will become a blessing to the whole creation."

When we name something (or someone) we not only affix to it identity and uniqueness, we empower it. Behaviorists tell us that it is not until we name our fears, anxieties, concerns, and problems that we can confront them. Conversely, it is not until we name and articulate our hopes, dreams, and aspirations that we can be empowered to achieve them. Naming instills not only particularization but also empowerment. Names both describe reality and create reality—what we are named and how we are described shape us.

> Our true identity is flat and plain, not puffed up with the wrong kind of ingredient. The Messiah, our Passover Lamb, has already been sacrificed for the Passover meal, and we are the Unraised Bread part of the Feast. So let's live out our part in the Feast, not as raised bread swollen with the yeast of evil, but as flat bread—simple, genuine, unpretentious.
>
> —I Corinthians 5:5–8

"Community of Christ" is not simply a name we claim—it claims us! It reminds us that Christ's ministry is broader, deeper, and far greater than the measure of our understandings and denomination. It is a name that calls us to "discern and embrace its full meaning" on the sacred journey to fulfill God's dream to bless creation. It challenges us to "live out our part in the Feast" by blessing others and the created order through "simple, genuine, and unpretentious" ministries that bear God's unconditional love.

Unique to Section 163 is its ecological (or perhaps better stated "wholistic") emphasis: "You will become a blessing to the whole creation." Our misguided anthropocentrism has misinterpreted God's blessing to "Be fruitful and multiply, and fill the earth and subdue it, and have dominion…over every living thing that moves upon the earth" (Genesis 1:28RSV). The Hebrew *radah* (to rule or have dominion) also means "to manage" or "to take responsibility for," denoting our pastoral responsibility to care for creation.

"Do not be afraid to go where it beckons you to go."

The counsel to not fear where our emerging identity leads us is a call to faithfulness—a willingness to let God *be* God. This mandate is not new. The phrase "do not be afraid" occurs forty-four times in the Hebrew Bible and eighteen times in the New Testament. It is the preface phrase in the first Christian homily: "*Do not be afraid*; for see—I am bringing you good news of great joy for all the people: to you is born this day in the city of David a Savior, who is the Messiah, the Lord" (Luke 2:10, NRSV).

It seems we need constant reassurance as we proceed along faith's path. And rightly so. At times, our need for stability and security has caused us to pound our tent posts deeply into the soil of cherished understandings and beliefs while at the same time we have searched for expanded understandings of God's purposes.

In response to the pervasive influence of the Holy Spirit we have seen shadows of disagreement dissolve over issues regarding baptisms in polygamist cultures, the ordination of women, close Communion, and the very name by which this movement bears its witness. These have not come without cost. The question is. "Are we willing to go beyond where we presently are?" Are we willing to confess our propensity to shape our beliefs into immaculate perceptions? Are we willing to enter uncharted fields of ministry to the lost, lonely, and labeled? Are we willing to broaden and deepen our understandings of ethnic, cultural, gender, political, and environmental issues? Are we willing to be taught as well as to teach?

A people open to revelation's transforming voice must be willing to be surprised. If God cannot surprise us then our God is too small. Despite a stormy history that has seen us cling to, then let go of, one cherished understanding after another, we have stayed the course of theological exploration. "The Truth must dazzle gradually," writes Emily Dickinson, "Or every man be blind." The motto inscribed on the library at *Virginia Theological Seminary*, accurately describes our sacred journey: "Seek the truth; come whence it may, lead where it will, cost what it may."

Ours is a rich heritage. We cherish the contributions of those who came before us. We are a martyred church having endured rejection, abuse, and the specter of literal extermination. We have strived to restore that which was lost or wanting. There is much we need to explore and understand about our denominational journey and that of the early Christian church. We continue to be blessed by history's lessons. Nevertheless, we are not called to resurrect the past—the horizon we are called to look beyond is not behind us.

It seems that religion is the only discipline that seeks its purity in the past. We are called to honor the past and create God's future. Marjorie Suchocki describes the reign of God as a state of unrest. "If the reign of God is always a principle of unrest, daring us to reverse previous values for the sake of greater well-being," she writes, "then the reign of God is that which calls us to dare a new future."[5]

Eugene H. Peterson's The Message (a contemporary translation of the Bible from the original languages) gives the well-known verse "perfect love casts out fear" (1 John 4:18) an interesting rendering:

> **God is love. When we take up permanent residence in a life of love, we live in God and God lives in us. This way, love has the run of the house, becomes at home and mature in us, so that we're free of worry…. There is no room in love for fear.**

In a very real sense the challenge to go where our identity leads us is to let "love have the run of the house"—to trust in that Spirit that leads to do good.

Although inspired counsel is given to the church, its timeless principles are applicable beyond the church. We live in troubled times. For many wounded souls, fear—not love—has the run of the house. Section 163 reminds us that we are called to reach out to those who yearn for the sanctuary of a loving community where acceptance and compassion rule. We are to be a community of hope and solace that will not sit in judgment of their actions but will compassionately befriend, defend, and seek to understand them.

In summary, the challenge "do not be afraid to go where it beckons you to go" is at the very core of who we are as a prophetic people. We cannot sing with integrity, "We limit not the truth of God to our poor reach or mind" or the chorus, "The Lord hath yet more light and truth to break forth from his word," if our best understandings are couched in beliefs and practices that have no breathing room. We remain open to inspired counsel. A faith that is finished—indeed, a faith not in ferment—is not faith at all. Ours is faith on the move—a faith that beckons us to go beyond where we are, to

---

5 Marjorie Hewitt Suchocki, Divinity & Diversity: A Christian Affirmation of Religious Pluralism (Nashville: Abingdon Press, 2003), 81

dream new dreams, to hope new hopes, to be Christ's community in daring and uncomfortable ways. We are being called to go deeper—to mine greater understanding of discipleship and to do so unafraid, trusting in that Spirit that shapes and blesses us by the very name we claim and that claims us: Community of Christ!

Paragraph 1: Questions for Reflection and Discussion

1. **Discernment Exercise**: Find a quiet place. Sit silently for several minutes. Empty your mind of concerns and distracting voices. Acknowledge you are in the presence of the Holy. Read paragraph 1 **several times** aloud or silently. Do so without searching for its meaning or interpretation. Simply read it repeatedly and allow the text to **choose you**. Close the text and sit silently for a short period. What words or phrases begin to surface? With pen and pad write down whatever insights or thoughts come to mind.

2. What is the derivation of your surname? How has your ethnicity and family heritage informed your personality? Do you like or dislike your first name? How has it shaped your sense of identity? Have you been given a "nick-name"? How has your name shaped who you are?

3. The church was renamed "Community of Christ" in 2001. What was your initial reaction when this name was proposed to the church? Does our name reflect in any way our denominational heritage and history? If so, how? If not, why not? What response do you receive from others when you tell interested parties the name of the church?

4. What does the phrase "discern and embrace its full meaning" say to you?

5. Although the church has members in more than fifty countries, we are a relatively small Christian denomination. Discuss how it would be possible for the church to become "a blessing to the whole creation."

6. In recent decades our church has undergone dramatic changes, for example, open Communion, ordination of women, a change in leadership lineage, adoption of a new name, the restructuring of field and headquarters design, broader interpretation of stewardship. The counsel "Do not be afraid to go where it beckons you to go" promises that challenge and change await us. Discuss your response to this challenge and the author's statement "We are not called to resurrect the past—the horizon we are called to look beyond is not behind us."

7. Discuss the following quotations:

   • "The Truth must dazzle gradually, Or every man be blind."—Emily Dickinson

   • "Seek the truth; come whence it may, lead where it will, cost what it may."—Inscribed on the library at Virginia Theological Seminary

Worship Helps—Paragraph One
Worship Reading

Reader One: I am yours and you are mine. I know your highest hopes—your deepest desires—for I have planted them in your hearts. Seek to discover and release them. I have called, claimed, and named you. The world hungers for sacred community. Open yourselves to its deeper meanings.

Reader Two: Open our eyes to your wonders, our ears to your still small voice, our will to your will. Guide our steps beyond the known. Let us live *forward*. Bless us with hope and courage as we give life to the name you have given us.

Reader One: *The creation aches for renewal. You are its hands, its feet, its voice. All life is sacred. I have placed its future under your feet. Tread softly, for it is part of my community. Salvation for one without salvation for all is salvation for none. The earth groans for liberation; bless it as it blesses you—for you are it and it is you.*

Reader Two: We have taken your name upon us. It is more than we are. We will move to where it beckons us, free of fear, responding to its call for a community that embraces all creation as sacred.

Prayer of Petition

God, you have called, claimed, and named us.

From wooded grove to swirling spire

   you have guided our faltering steps.

You have wept in our weakness

   and rejoiced in our strength.

You have swept aside shadows of doubt,

   forgiven our reluctance to let go of lesser things,

   and challenged us with new horizons.

Bless us to truly be a community

   that bears your Son's name.

Open our hearts, minds, and will to its call.

May its circumference encircle all

   who seek joy, hope, love, and peace.

May it define us and redefine us.

May it bless your wounded earth,

   setting at liberty creatures great and small.

Free us from fear as we discover more fully

   who you are calling us to become

   —a faithful witness of Christ's community

   in daily word and deed. Amen.

Christ Bids Our Hearts to Sail

8.6.8.6.8.6.8.6

Tune: BETHLEHEM (SERAPH) (*Hymns of the Saints* # 435)
Alternative Tune: ELLACOMBE (*HS* # 471)

The hidden seas within the soul Christ bids our hearts to sail.

To face the winds and waves of change, With courage to prevail.

To cast away from safety's shore Unfettered by our fear

And float on faith above the storm, Assured that Christ is near.

To deeper depths Christ beckons us, Our calling to discern;

With winds of hope to stir our quest, To understand and learn.

Content no more in shallow streams, Our purpose to explore

The truth of who we're called to be, Down deep within faith's core.

The name of Christ defines our call—It shapes our destiny

To share the vision of God's peace as Christ's community,

Whose common task—with cultures vast—Creation can redeem.

We hold the keys to plot the course to realize God's dream.

Paragraph 2:
The Embodiment of Shalom

2 a. Jesus Christ, the embodiment of God's shalom, invites all people to come and receive divine peace in the midst of the difficult questions and struggles of life. Follow Christ in the way that leads to God's peace and discover the blessings of all of the dimensions of salvation.

"Jesus Christ, the embodiment of God's shalom…"

The Hebrew word *shalom* escapes adequate translation in English. Commonly used by our Jewish sisters and brothers to say "hello" and "good-bye" as a blessing of peace, it conveys far more than a wish for freedom from strife and disorder. Shalom has many more meanings than the word "peace" in English. Strong's Concordance, a word study in the New King James version, says for "shalom": "Completeness, wholeness, health, peace, welfare, safety soundness, tranquility, prosperity, perfectness, fullness, rest, harmony, the absence of agitation or discord."

Shalom conveys friendship, well-being, safety, and salvation. The apostle Paul understood the "*shalom, shalom*" of Isaiah 57:19 (*Peace, peace*, to the far and the near, says the Lord; and I will heal them.) as a reference to salvation, not just peace. He makes it clear that Jesus is the embodiment of shalom when he says that Jesus is our "shalom," our peace, and our salvation.

> For he is our peace; in his flesh he has made both groups into one and has broken down the dividing wall, that is, the hostility between us. He has abol-

ished the law with its commandments and ordinances, that he might create in himself one new humanity in place of the two, thus making peace, and might reconcile both groups to God in one body through the cross, thus putting to death that hostility through it. So he came and proclaimed peace to you who were far off and peace to those who were near; for through him both of us have access in one Spirit to the Father. So then you are no longer strangers and aliens, but you are citizens with the saints and also members of the household of God

—Ephesians 2:14–18 NRSV

"…come and receive divine peace in the midst of the difficult questions and struggles of life."

Shalom must have hands and feet. As the "embodiment" of God's shalom, Jesus invites all people to receive the blessings of divine peace "in the midst of the difficult questions and struggles of life." The peace of Jesus, then, is not necessarily the absence of trouble or tribulation, but the active presence of shalom (peace) in the midst of life's unevenness.

Life continually challenges us with difficult, heart-rending decisions. The spirit of shalom says we must be willing to "receive divine peace in the midst" of these challenges—to step back and take a breath, to listen carefully, to not rush to predetermined judgments that favor what we *think* we know, and what we *think* is right as the cost of what *is* right. Our hardened viewpoints can break *us* as well as others if not softened by receiving the gift of divine peace. We must resist living a dialectic absent of doubt. The opposite of faith is not doubt—the opposite of faith is fear. We must be willing to question our faith. We of all people have learned that certitude yields to idolatry.

The peace we seek is God's peace, not our peace. God's peace passes understanding—it is never static. It is not some hoped-for Utopia, nor is it a glass of lemonade, a hammock, palm trees, and soft ocean breezes on a sleepy sunny afternoon. There is a difference between being at peace and being *at* peace! Someone said "Those seeking a permanent stable condition will be doomed to disappointment—God's peace has to do with personhood, not property or comfort or convenience, or ambience." It has to do with personhood that recognizes the inestimable worth of each soul and their interconnectivity, the mutuality of life that inspires loving response and sacrifices for those whose plight or circumstance is wanting. God's peace is never a negative state, never just the absence of trouble.

Peace cannot perform its function as long as it exists in splendid isolation. Peace is a noun crying to be a verb! To paraphrase Daniel Day Williams:

> [Peace] does not put everything to rest; it puts everything in motion. [Peace] does not end all risks; it accepts every risk that is necessary for its work. [Peace] does not resolve every conflict. It accepts conflict as the arena in which the work of [peace] must be done. [Peace] does not neatly separate the good people from the bad—[peace] seeks the reconciliation of every life...so that it may share with all others.[6]

Shalom, when embodied, involves everything that makes for one's highest good. It means not evading issues; it means facing them, dealing with them, conquering them. It's realizing that peace for me alone is not peace at all! Peacemaking is never-ending. It calls for dealing with the greatest enemies of shalom—indifference and ignorance. It has been said that "a faith that does nothing and costs nothing and suffers nothing is worth nothing!"[7]

"...discover the blessings of all of the dimensions of salvation."

This line of text challenges us to explore salvation's deeper meanings—to free it from the confines of eschatological blessings "there and then" to its blessings in the "here and now." Traditionally, we have been reticent in sharing our witness of what is called the "doctrine of Christian assurance." The statement "I am saved" for many in our denomination would be amended quickly to, "I *may* be saved, *if* I am faithful."

The core meaning of the doctrine of Christian assurance is that salvation is not exclusively future oriented—it testifies of the unwavering acceptance of God's grace in our lives here and now. It says we are assured of God's love because it is a gift. God's love is unconditional, uncaused, unmerited, unrelenting. It is groundless. It is love that is always seeking, but not requiring. A love that is never arbitrary, whimsical, or withdrawn. It is love without strings attached. As recipients of love unearned we are transformed to love others likewise.

We have made sin the exclusive focus of salvation, whereas sin is not the sole problem of the human condition. Salvation means, among other things, "to be set in an open space"—to be liberated from physical, mental, and spiritual impairments prohibiting fullness of life. Paragraph 2 urges us to discover dimensions of salvation that provide forgiveness for the enemy, haven for the refugee, liberation for the oppressed, food for the hungry, and a just society for all.

As made clear later in Section 163, the dimensions of salvation encompass the created order. The earth cries to be set free from the silent war we have waged on ecology. It yearns for salvation, renewal, and rebirth here and now (see paragraph 4).

---

2 b. Generously share the invitation, ministries, and sacraments through which people can encounter the Living Christ who heals and reconciles through redemptive relationships in sacred community. The restoring of persons to healthy or righteous relationships with God, others, themselves, and the earth is at the heart of the purpose of your journey as a people of faith.

"Generously share the invitation, ministries, and sacraments..."

Generosity is our joyful response to God's generosity toward us. Its governing spirit is not formulas but thankfulness. Generosity always wants to do more—it moves us from minimums to maximums, from law to life, from obligation to opportunity.

We who have been blessed by the ministries and sacraments of the church are counseled, once again, to share these blessings abundantly with others and to extend this invitation without reservation. Reticence to invite others may be fueled by fear of rejection or the mistaken presumption that he or she would not be in-

---

[6] See Daniel Day Williams, *The Spirit and Forms of Love* (New York: Harper and Row, 1968) 138. I have substituted the word "peace" in place of "love."
[7] Source unknown.

terested. When we "generously share the invitation" we do so joyfully, permitting them to decide for themselves. Many in need of blessings wait only for an invitation. Conversely, many who have talents and gifts of ministry to offer the church await our invitation to do so. We have been counseled:

> Look especially to the sacraments to enrich the spiritual life of the body. Seek for greater understanding of my purposes in these sacred rites and prepare to receive a renewed confirmation of the presence of my Spirit in your experiences of worship.
> —Doctrine and Covenants 158:11c

> But be neither captive to time-bound formulas and procedures. Remember that instruction given in former years is applicable in principle and must be measured against the needs of a growing church, in accordance with the prayerful direction of the spiritual authorities and the consent of the people.
> —Doctrine and Covenants 161:5

Sacraments involve covenant—a mutuality of "gift and response." God always blesses us through the sacraments, but a blessing must be received and appropriated. For example, bread and wine can be blessed and served, but if worshipers are *not* giving themselves (that is, purposefully discerning the meaning of these emblems) *sacrament* will not take place and the extension of this blessing beyond the worship experience and community will be short-lived.

> The ordinances and sacraments employ all of our faculties to allow God to disclose to us the nature of reality. They allow us to express most fully our devotion and commitment. God who has created us and said, "All things which I had made were very good," speaks to our whole being in the ordinances. We respond physically, emotionally, intellectually, socially, because our response to God is total. We are involved in physical action, drama, and speech in ways which cause us to understand most accurately what it is that God is requiring of us and what it means to yield our lives to Christ and be a new person… The sacraments are an extension of the ministry of incarnation in which God uses human nature and material things to express godliness tangibly in humankind….We are involved mentally as we understand the meaning of the sacrament. We respond physically in the acts which dramatize the meaning of our covenants. We respond emotionally and we are linked with the church spiritually and socially in participating with the groups which make up the body.[8]

The blessings of these rites extend beyond the rites themselves. Participation in the sacraments (as with all liturgical acts) presupposes that there will be a change in understanding, attitude, and behavior by the worshiper. Worship is not an escape from reality but a means to awaken us to reality. Section 163 reminds us that such blessings and ministries are not intended to be exhausted upon ourselves but, by extension and invitation, are a means to bless creation.

"…through which people can encounter the Living Christ who heals and reconciles through redemptive relationships in sacred community."

Redemption is not a private affair. One can certainly have a personal encounter with the Living Christ, but healing and reconciliation for *me* and *mine* are *not* complete until there is healing and reconciliation for *you* and *yours*. Religious privatism is the empty promise of a parochial god.

Healing and reconciliation are the blessings of "redemptive relationships in sacred community." The hallmark of sacred community is spiritual formation. Community is made sacred through anamnesis—"collective sacred memory"—which assimilates God's unconditional love made manifest through scripture, tradition, reason, and experience and "lived out" in community.

Collective sacred memory is not memory in the traditional sense—it is not vicarious recall of the past of the experiences of others. When our Jewish sisters and brothers celebrate Passover they rejoice that *they themselves* (not just their ancestors) have been brought out of bondage. Collective memory, then, is a lively awareness or active awakening of God's grace expressed personally and corporately in the *here* and *now* cemented by the bonds of a loving community. At times we become *dis-membered* from self, others, and God. Collective memory (the prayerful support, care, and witness of a sacred community) serves to *re-member* or restore us to rightful relationships.

Such a community then is not merely a cooperative collection of individuals who agree to live civilly together. Sacred community is governed by its willingness to confess its weaknesses in love and to labor to ensure the worth and redemption of each soul—indeed, the very creation. Sacred community seeks to transform inequitable social structures that privilege the few and deny the many—it is where the bruised and brokenhearted are blessed and none are marginalized by gender, age, race, sexual orientation, or philosophy. It is not a one-size fits all society but emerges within cultural contexts centered in joy, hope, love, and peace; it is life blessed by diversity without conformity and made harmonious

---

[8] *The Priesthood Manual* (Independence, Missouri: Herald Publishing House, 1982), 205–207.

by its common denominator—a lively witness of God's grace.

"The restoring of persons to healthy or righteous relationships with God, others, themselves, and the earth is at the heart of the purpose of your journey as a people of faith."

Life is relationships. We have barely crossed the threshold of a postmodern worldview where quantum physics is redefining perceptions of reality. The word "universe" in a sense is reclaiming its root meaning, i.e., "one reality" in that all that *was*, *is*, and *will be* and is inexplicably connected or *one*. There is no sharp dividing line between the sacred and the secular. As the Qumran texts remind us, we are the product of a very special union—"a *sacred marriage* between the soul of the heavens and the tissue of the world."[9]

We relate to our past, the present, the anticipated future, others, self, God, and a myriad of complex relationships wrapped up in the very cosmos itself. We are not only shaped by these relationships, we shape them for good or ill. The gospel calls for the right or *righteous* arrangement of relationships. Accordingly, paragraph 2 challenges us to be about the task of restoring healthy relationships, which is "at the heart of the purpose" of our faith journey.

Out of sheer joy, we, who are so richly blessed, can do no other. We are called to respond not only to the plight of those trapped by circumstance and poor choice, but to respond to the cries of the earth for deliverance and new birth. Life is not a solo act; its tapestry is multifaceted. We are woven together with diverse threads and all are God's chosen fabric!

---

[9] As quoted by Gregg Braden, *The Isaiah Effect* (New York: Three Rivers Press, 2000), 44.

Paragraph 2: Questions for Reflection and Discussion

1. Discernment Exercise: Find a quiet place. Sit silently for several minutes. Empty your mind of concerns and distracting voices. Acknowledge you are in the presence of the Holy. Read paragraph 2 several times aloud or silently. Do so without searching for its meaning or interpretation. Simply read it repeatedly and allow the text to choose you. Close the text and sit silently for a short period. What words or phrases begin to surface? With pen and pad write down whatever insights or thoughts come to mind.

2. When have you received divine peace in the midst of difficult questions and struggles?

3. Paragraph 2 instructs us to "Follow Christ in the way that leads to God's peace." What does it mean to follow Christ "in the way"?

4. Discuss the following statements from page 19: "God's peace is not our peace" and "peace is never a negative state, never just the absence of trouble."

5. Paragraph 2 challenges us to "discover the blessings of all of the dimensions of salvation." What is your understanding of salvation?

6. Group Discernment Exercise: "Generously share the invitation, ministries, and sacraments." Sit quietly for a few minutes contemplating the names of people who have influenced your faith journey. When all have had time to meditate, randomly begin to speak some of these names aloud in the group in a spirit of reverence and thanksgiving.

7. Whose generous invitation made it possible for you to share Christ's ministry with others?

8. Share an experience when participation in a sacrament had special significance in your life.

9. Discuss the commentator's statements: "Sacraments involve covenant—a mutuality of 'gift and response.'… The blessings of these rites extend beyond the rites themselves."

10. It has been said that nothing is so secular that it cannot be sacred. What makes community sacred as opposed to secular? Reflect on the phrase "sacred community." In a world of diverse political systems and cultures, what common principles ("right relationships") would need to be in place to distinguish a community as being sacred?

Worship Helps—Paragraph 2

Litany Based on
Doctrine and Covenants 163:2

Leader: *I walk the streets in ragged clothes. I'm on the bus beside you. I laugh and run in children's shoes. I am old and young. I'm stout. I'm thin. I'm everywhere that life begins and ends. My Spirit lives within you.*

Congregation: ***Help us to see your hidden face in every soul we meet today. Help us to be your living peace—your hands, your feet, your gentle voice that speaks release to all who seek shalom.***

Leader: *I yearn to save my groaning earth, the lost, the torn, the fractured souls who cry for worth. Salvation's more than sin's release. It finds the lost. It offers peace. It feeds the poor. It liberates. It guides the lost. It opens hearts. It heals, redeems, and reconciles. It walks and talks shalom.*

Congregation: ***Help us to see your hidden face in every soul we meet today. Help us to be your living peace—your hands, your feet, your gentle voice that speaks release to all who seek shalom.***

----

[10] See Marcus J. Borg, *The Heart of Christianity* (HarperSanFrancisco, New York: 2003), 168.

Prayer of Petition

God, sin is overrated.

Not the deed (or deeds)—the concept.

Three letters. One syllable.

This short insufferable sound stuffed with eternal damnation.

Enough to go around for everyone.

Too much self-analysis bankrupts the soul.

It's sinful what we've done with the word "sin," God.

We have crowned it salvation's cause célèbre

    when we need saving from so much more.

It is good news, indeed, to be forgiven,

    but the gospel's bigger than that.

And so are you, God.

Misdeeds and "missed deeds" are not our only problem.

Borg said it best:

    "When I am blind, I need to see.

    When I am in exile, I need to return.

    When I am in bondage, I need liberation.

    When I have a closed heart, I need it opened.

    When I hunger and thirst, I need food and drink.

    When I can't find my way, I need to be found."[10]

Help us, God, to see the deeper dimensions of salvation.

May we not hang its blessings on some distant star or place,

    but live its peace, here and now.

May we generously share its blessings with all

    who seek your shalom. Amen.

When Christ Embodied God's Shalom

8.6.8.6.8.6.8.6

Tune: FOREST GREEN (*Hymns of the Saints* #484)
ELLACOMBE (*HS* #471)

When Christ embodied God's shalom He blessed a world in need

That suffered from disunity And struggled to be freed.

Dimensions of salvation's grace Exceed the blight of sin—

The hungry fed, the lost are found, the captive freed within.

Shalom is just a breath away—Its life depends on you.

Your hands, your feet, your voice it seeks—It comes alive in you—

Restoring right relationships By sharing hope and care

Through ministries and sacraments the Living Christ we share.

Shalom is not a word or phrase—It's everything we do

To calm the stormy seas of life—To bless the earth anew.

Its heartbeat is our faithful quest For God's community,

To heal, redeem, and reconcile estranged humanity.

Personify the peace of Christ—The gift of God's shalom.

Help those who face perplexities Who seek a sacred home.

Swing wide the doors of charity Inviting all to be

Embraced by Christ's community with love and harmony.

Notes

Paragraph 3: Pathways for Peace

3 a. You are called to create pathways in the world for peace in Christ to be relationally and culturally incarnate. The hope of Zion is realized when the vision of Christ is embodied in communities of generosity, justice, and peacefulness.

b. Above all else, strive to be faithful to Christ's vision of the peaceable Kingdom of God on earth. Courageously challenge cultural, political, and religious trends that are contrary to the reconciling and restoring purposes of God. Pursue peace.

c. There are subtle, yet powerful, influences in the world, some even claiming to represent Christ, that seek to divide people and nations to accomplish their destructive aims. That which seeks to harden one human heart against another by constructing walls of fear and prejudice is not of God. Be especially alert to these influences, lest they divide you or divert you from the mission to which you are called.

"You are called to create pathways in the world for peace in Christ to be relationally and culturally incarnate."

The text calls us to create pathways, reminding us that there are many paths in the world for peace that are not only possible but necessary. Creating a pathway is not only hard work, but requires discernment and a willingness to *suspend disbelief.* It calls for exploration and discovery—a leap of faith, where the familiar is left behind and we push ahead not knowing what challenges, disappointments, and resistance we may encounter. It is a journey through the unknown *toward* the known. We know where we want to go but we may have to experiment on how best to get there.

Faith is not a destination; it is a direction. Our hopes, dreams, and aspirations are in direct ratio to our willingness to put our feet down where they have yet to tread. We subtly slip into predictability and sameness. The *everydayness* of life can rob us of God's whisper in our lives. We can be so caught up in the way things are, we forget how things once were and how much better things can be. We are tempted to return to the familiar when God's journey calls us forward into the unknown, untested, and unfamiliar. We must not retreat to what used to be and resist what could be. Our faith journey calls us to make a positive difference, to somehow erase the dividing line between the sacred and the secular—to make the gospel a *live option*!

Peace in Christ is "to be relationally and culturally incarnate." In a world of religious and cultural diversity we must jettison parochial perceptions that we and we alone have the answers. The weight of U.S. and Canadian membership in the church should not delude us into thinking that inside every foreign national is a Canadian or U.S. citizen trying to get out. Similarly, there is not a "Community of Christ membership" striving to be claimed inside those of other faiths. Jesus applauded the good works of those who were not his followers or disciples. The declaration "The hope of Zion is realized when the *vision* of Christ is embodied in communities of generosity, justice, and peacefulness" hints that this hope and task extends beyond Christianity itself. Many of our sisters and brothers of other faiths share Christ's *vision* of a peaceable kingdom.

Creating pathways of peace, then, is a *give* and *take* journey wherein we must honor nuanced foundational principles of peace dressed in various cultural clothes and religions—a mutual sharing and expanding of Christ's *vision of peace* that is exciting and enriching. Success in navigating this journey will correspond with our desire to make every pathway an Emmaus road, where each stranger (Christian or non-Christian) with whom we walk is a *reflection* of the peace of Jesus.

"…strive to be faithful to Christ's vision of the peaceable Kingdom of God on earth. Courageously challenge cultural, political, and religious trends that are contrary to the reconciling and restoring purposes of God."

"Above all else, strive to be faithful to Christ's vision of the peaceable Kingdom…" Can there be a clearer call to be a prophetic people than the call to courageously challenge demeaning and destructive "cultural, political, and religious trends"? Prophetic ministry is truth-telling. It is hope-telling. It is a clear and compelling witness (word and deed) that unswervingly confronts laws, systems, and attitudes that dwarf and diminish the created order. Biblical prophets boldly addressed the peace and justice issues of their day. Their prophetic ministry was not focused primarily in predictive possibilities but in discerning and voicing God's response to the unevenness of the times in which they lived, and they did so in no uncertain terms. Loyalty to (or fear of) political powers held no sway. Their only patriotism was patriotism to a moral compass aligned to God's will and way.

We tend to default to a comfortable gospel that meekly and mildly tells people what they want to hear. There is not much good news in a gospel that lacks size! Every social change for the common good has emerged from a people of faith who have bravely put their beliefs and convictions on the line. We are called to do no less—to tear down walls of division regardless of their height, grandeur, and do-good promises. We must no longer succumb to the blindness of our own biases and prejudices whether these be religious, racial, political, gender, or sexually based. Walls that keep people in are the same walls that keep people out.

The commission to courageously challenge trends that hinder "God's reconciling and restoring purposes" is double-sided. It is not enough to criticize or speak out against such destructive influences. We are called to eradicate them through ministries and programs. We must be *for* something as well *against* something. To effectively challenge demeaning attitudes, policies, and actions we must present practical and powerful alternatives and vigorously advocate for their realization.

"There are subtle, yet powerful, influences in the world, some even claiming to represent Christ, that seek to divide people and nations…"

This sentence sounds an alarm far exceeding the common adage "Beware of wolves in sheep's clothing." A prophetic people must be a discerning people. We are cautioned to prayerfully examine and challenge programs, institutions, and yes, even ministries labeled "Christian" whose ends are self-serving and destructive. Many people (and nations) in dire need fall prey to unscrupulous schemes promising aid and relief.

North America is no exception. Some social commentators suggest that, despite our affluence, we are dwelling in a culture of fear exacerbated by threats of terrorism on our doorstep. Force, power, and military might are no longer a last resort, and preemptive war is wrapped in a lexicon of "liberation," "defeating evildoers," and "defending our interests." We have seen personal freedoms diminish by regulations deemed necessary to protect us. Security can be neither purchased nor guaranteed by governments and safety programs. Our only security is discerning what is right and acting on it. As a prophetic people we are called to be in the forefront of those movements committed to eradicating negative activities and influences that devalue the worth of souls and the created order.

Paragraph 3: Questions for Reflection and Discussion

1. **Discernment Exercise**: Find a quiet place. Sit silently for several minutes. Empty your mind of concerns and distracting voices. Acknowledge you are in the presence of the Holy. Read paragraph 3 **several times** aloud or silently. Do so without searching for its meaning or interpretation. Simply read it repeatedly and allow the text to **choose you**. Close the text and sit silently for a short period. What words or phrases begin to surface? With pen and pad write down whatever insights or thoughts come to mind.

2. "You are called to create pathways in the world for peace in Christ…" How might this be done in your congregation? We need not look to distant shores to respond to this question. As of this writing there are more than 400 homeless children in the Independence, Missouri, school system. What needs exist in your community and what pathways for peace cry out to be created? Finally, how might you create pathways of peace within the sphere of your personal influence?

3. Peace in Christ is "to be relationally and culturally incarnate." Discuss the commentator's statement "In a world of religious and cultural diversity we must jettison parochial perceptions that we and we alone have the answers." What pathways of peace can be created to bridge religious and cultural differences within and beyond the church?

4. The hymn "Great Is Thy Faithfulness" (*Hymns of the Saints* #187) reminds us that God has faith in us. Paragraph 3b declares, "Above all else, strive to be faithful to Christ's vision of the peaceable Kingdom of God on earth." When has your faith been tested and what held you firm in the midst of questioning and doubt? In what ways has your faith changed through the years? Is the establishment of the peaceable kingdom exclusively a Christian pursuit?

5. We are to courageously challenge trends contrary to the restoring purposes of God. Challenging such trends requires not only verbally challenging them but taking positive action to offset them. In your opinion what are some cultural, political, and religious trends that need to be addressed, and in what way?

6. People's hearts harden when their beliefs become "immaculate perceptions." They refuse to listen to other points of view because theirs and theirs alone is the only way. Discuss paragraph 3c: "That which seeks to harden one human heart against another by constructing walls of fear and prejudice is not of God. Be especially alert to these influences, lest they divide you from the mission to which you are called." Walls of distrust and misunderstanding can be erected quickly and subtly. What have you done when this has happened to you? Have you purposely or unwittingly put up a wall of resistance to another?

Worship Helps—Paragraph 3

Leader: *You have only tasted the blessings of peace. Fuller dimensions and expressions of its grace are before you. They await exploration and discovery. My peace has many faces: black, brown, white, and yellow; young and old, rich and poor. The time for hesitation has passed. Create new pathways. Open new doors.*

All: **Horizons of hope call to us. We will place our feet where they have yet to tread. We will be your people, God.**

Leader: *Many wander in disbelief seduced by subtle forces imitating my gospel. Peace is frustrated by those who bend its meaning for self-serving purposes. Strengthen your resolve to speak for those who cannot speak and stand for those who cannot stand.*

All: **Horizons of hope call to us. We will not remain silent. We will be your people, God.**

Leader: *The hope of Zion is in your hands and the hands of all who share the vision of peace. My community of faith extends beyond the doors of your sanctuaries. Be faithful to your calling and unite your efforts with all who embody generosity, justice, and peacefulness.*

All: **Horizons of hope call to us. We will join hands in community with all who pursue your peace. We will be your people, God.**

Reading (or Prayer of Commitment): "Let Our Voices Rise"

God, we hear your call to pursue peace

    —to embody within us the principles of justice and grace.

You have placed the hope of Zion in our hands.

They are not equal to the task

    —for too often they have grasped lesser things.

Like sand sifting through uncupped hands,

    we have seen peace slip silently away

    —never fully realized—never made incarnate.

Forgive the detours of our faith.

Put us once again on its path,

    finding new avenues to realize your vision of community.

Grant us courage to challenge

    that which frustrates your purposes.

Awaken within us your call to be living sanctuaries

    of your peace—walking hand in hand with all

    who celebrate your many names.

May our voices rise above the hymns we sing,

    the prayers we pray, the sermons we preach.

May they be heard defending the used and abused.

May they speak out against the subtle influences

    that detract from your way.

And may they speak with gentleness, Lord,

    inviting every race and face

    to be your people.

God, Grant Us Courage

8.8.8.8.8.8.8.8

Tune: LAMB OF GOD (*Worship and Rejoice* # 503)
YE BANKS & BRAES (*Worship and Rejoice* #628)
DUANE STREET (*The Hymnal* #288)

God, grant us courage lest we fail To meet the challenge of this hour,

For fear assails our trembling will Whene'er we rest on our frail power.

We must not wait nor hesitate To raze the walls that segregate,

That harden hearts and amputate The peace of Christ we incarnate.

We are the hands and feet of peace—We are its voice that brings release

To those whose lives are victimized By trends and rules that minimize.

Speak now for those who cannot speak—Stand now for those who cannot stand.

Let nothing sway us from God's call To share the peace of Christ with all.

The church cannot confine its faith To pulpits, pews, and temple spires—

Swing wide its doors, create new paths Where justice walks and hope inspires.

Proclaim God's grace. Pursue God's peace. Confront the powers whose aims decrease

Zionic dreams through subtle schemes That claim Christ's name for their own means.

Above all else be faithful to The vision that Christ births in you

To realize God's peace on earth, Embodied in each culture's worth,

Where unity and harmony Are blessed by rich diversity—

Where love and generosity Prevail in each community.

Pursue the Peace of Christ

6.7.6.7.6.6.6.6.

Tune: NUN DANKET ALLE GOTT (*Hymns of the Saints* # 60)

Pursue the peace of Christ—Let justice be our anthem
Wrapped not in soothing words But in our daily actions—
For words divorced from deeds Like seeds upon the wind
Are scattered praise we raise That have no life within.

Pursue the peace of Christ—Let joy and laughter bring
God's healing balm of bliss Where hope no longer sings.
For day fades into night When faith is drained away—
Release the peace of Christ, Which turns our night to day.

Pursue the peace of Christ—At tables of Communion
Where bread and wine are shared As emblems of Christ's union.
This supper's grace extends To counter, bench, and desk
When blessed to share Christ's peace With all who are oppressed.

Pursue the peace of Christ—A peace beyond convention
That pierces terror's night With light and liberation.
A peace at war with hate—A peace that never rests
Till all creation shines And every soul is blessed.

Notes

Paragraph 4: In Their Welfare Resides Your Welfare

4 a. God, the Eternal Creator, weeps for the poor, displaced, mistreated, and diseased of the world because of their unnecessary suffering. Such conditions are not God's will. Open your ears to hear the pleading of mothers and fathers in all nations who desperately seek a future of hope for their children. Do not turn away from them. For in their welfare resides your welfare.

b. The earth, lovingly created as an environment for life to flourish, shudders in distress because creation's natural and living systems are becoming exhausted from carrying the burden of human greed and conflict. Humankind must awaken from its illusion of independence and unrestrained consumption without lasting consequences.

c. Let the educational and community development endeavors of the church equip people of all ages to carry the ethics of Christ's peace into all arenas of life. Prepare new generations of disciples to bring fresh vision to bear on the perplexing problems of poverty, disease, war, and environmental deterioration. Their contributions will be multiplied if their hearts are focused on God's will for creation.

"God, the Eternal Creator, weeps for the poor, displaced, mistreated, and diseased of the world because of their unnecessary suffering."

The first sentence of Scott Peck's *The Road Less Travelled* is "Life is difficult." Pain and suffering are part of existence and do not go unnoticed by God. Paragraph 4's depiction of God weeping for the poor, displaced, mistreated, and diseased is reminiscent of Isaiah's suffering servant passage: "Surely he has borne our infirmities and carried our diseases; yet we accounted him stricken, struck down by God, and afflicted" (Isaiah 53:4 RSV).

The phrase "unnecessary suffering" reminds us that all suffering is not detrimental. Some suffering is not only necessary—it is integrative and beneficial. Theologian Douglas John Hall (in *God and Human Suffering*, p. 65) distinguishes between suffering that is *necessary* (integrative suffering) and suffering that is *unnecessary* (disintegrative suffering). He maintains that the struggle to *become* who we are cannot be realized without pain: "There is a measure of pain in every sort of growth known to human science. *Becoming is suffering.*" Integrative suffering, then, serves life (e.g., physical pain that alerts us to problems, disciplines of self-denial, grief in response to loss, the struggles associated with the transition from childhood to adolescence, etc.). It is the *no pain/no gain* suffering of *becoming*—whereas, disintegrative suffering is destructive, detracting, and unnecessary.

We may say that it is…the distinction between the suffering which is necessary to creaturely becoming (integrative suffering) and suffering which detracts from life (disintegrative suffering)…what makes for life and what makes for death, what builds and what destroys, what enhances and what detracts.[11]

The focus of paragraph 4a is disintegrative suffering and our call to do something about it.

Whenever we consider suffering, the question of *theodicy* (i.e., the attempt to reconcile the existence of evil or suffering with the assumption of an omnipotent, benevolent God) raises its head. *Omnipotence* (the assumption that God could, if God chose, simply eliminate suffering) has its downside. Hall points out that this assumption is, in essence, a "limiting factor."

> When infinite power is posited as the primary and characteristic attribute of deity, then no one can be satisfied with an answer that is less than the abolition of suffering as such! It is the power assumption itself that must be questioned….The Judeo-Christian tradition does not *deny* the power of God, but neither does it magnify this attribute; moreover, and more to the point, it does not subtract the divine power from divine-human relationship. The relationship qualifies—radically—the nature and development of power on God's part.[12]

> To reiterate: there are situations where power is of no avail. *They are most of the situations in which as human beings we find ourselves!* May we not also dare to say that from the standpoint of a faith tradition which posits love, not power, as God's primary perfection, they are most of the situations in which God finds God's Self too?[13]

In other words, there are situations in which power simply doesn't work. Hall asks, "Who, through power tactics, can eliminate the self-destroying habits of a son or a daughter who has fallen prey to hard drugs? What nation, through power alone, can ensure world peace?… There is no sword that can cut away sin without killing the sinner" (p. 98).

Why does God not stop unnecessary suffering? The simple answer is, God cannot. Suffering resulting from personal (or corporate) self-serving interests and choices is our burden to bear. Freedom of choice is not freedom from the consequences of our choices. God weeps because the conditions referenced are *not* God's will and are *beyond* God's changing.

Some readers may hear the notes of *process theism*[14] humming mildly in the background of this response. Be that as it may, God has no hands and no feet other than our hands and feet. The vicissitudes of nature strike where they may; we have no control over wind, wave, earthquake, or storm. We *do* have control over what we say, the decisions we make, and the actions we take. The unnecessary suffering we are dealing with here is not God's doing; it is directly attributable to human-

ity's inhumanity—our inability (or unwillingness) to "open our ears" to those in desperate need.

Pain is proximate. My toothache dulls my ability to feel discomfort for faceless thousands who are homeless, starving, and abused—because it is *my* pain. Hall states it this way:

> Those who suffer most conspicuously in our society—the aged, the dying, the poor, the socially or psychically "abnormal"—are for the most part hidden from everyday view, sequestered in places which effectively insulate them from public notice; and the oppressed in our midst—racial minorities, sexual minorities, the unemployed, and others—can still seem to the majority of us to be well and wisely treated.[15]

"Open your ears to hear the pleading of mothers and fathers in all nations who desperately seek a future of hope for their children…in their welfare resides your welfare."

The phrases "the pleading of mothers and fathers" and "a future of hope for their children" paint the face of parenthood on the faceless and shrink the comfortable distance between we who may not be in distress with those who are. The central issue here is *connectivity*, while the more specific focus (though not specifically stated) is *community* ("Do not turn away from them. For in their welfare resides your welfare"). God's tears are our tears; our tears are God's tears. Another's pain is our pain; the earth's pain is our pain. Paragraph 4 is clearly a call to action! We cannot remain silent and uninvolved.

> First they came for the communists, and I did not speak out—because I was not a communist. Then they came for the socialists, and I did not speak out—because I was not a socialist. Then they came for the Jews, and I did not speak out—because I was not a Jew. Then they came for me—and there was no one left to speak for me.
> —Rev. Martin Niemoller, 1945

---

[11] Douglas John Hall, *God & Human Suffering: An Exercise in the Theology of the Cross* (Augsburg Press, 1986), 67–68.

[12] Hall, *God & Human Suffering*, 97.

[13] Ibid., 99.

[14] Process theology suggests that everything, including God, is in process. The future is open and God is doing all God can do to bring about good, but God's power is persuasive not coercive.

[15] Hall, *God & Human Suffering*, 26.

> b. The earth, lovingly created as an environment for life to flourish, shudders in distress because creation's natural and living systems are becoming exhausted from carrying the burden of human greed and conflict. Humankind must awaken from its illusion of independence and unrestrained consumption without lasting consequences.

We are slowly awakening to ecological emergencies that have been hammering at our door for decades. "The earth groans for the liberating truths of my gospel" is not a poetic phrase but a revelatory warning that, for the most part, we have failed to heed. "There is enough and to spare" is not a "ticket to ride" or a divine declaration of inexhaustible natural resources awaiting our unbridled consumption. "Humankind must awaken from its delusion of independence." The principles of community and interrelationship are inherent in all that has been, all that is, and all that will be.

We have forgotten that we are stardust. We have permitted anthropocentrism to rule by placing humanity on the highest rung of creation's ladder, failing to realize we are but *part* of the ladder. All life is interdependent—relationally co-existent. We *are* the earth (the cosmos) *thinking, talking,* and *walking*—an expression of the created order whose degree of consciousness enjoys a wider arena of freedom (and moral aptitude) than plants and other animals. Paragraph 4b is an extension of the counsel that precedes it, namely, the admonition that *our welfare* is inseparable from the *earth's welfare*. In this sense, we are not stewards *over* the earth, but stewards *with* the earth in the on-going stream of creation. But our penchant to serve our own selfish ends now threatens life as we know it and life as it should be. This admonition echoes previous counsel to the church in Doctrine and Covenants 150:7:

> These are portentous times. The lives of many are being sacrificed unnecessarily to the gods of war, greed, and avarice. The land is being desecrated by the thoughtless waste of vital resources. You must obey my commandments and be in the forefront of those who would mediate this needless destruction while there is yet day.

We yearn for Zion, the peaceable kingdom. Yet distorted concepts of Zion can exacerbate ecological problems. Unhealthy emphasis on heaven or "the afterlife," for some Christians, has fostered an attitude that life in the *here and now* is but a rehearsal existence, a pale foretaste of the glory that awaits us after death or when God will make a new heaven and a new earth.

Such attitudes cultivate apathy and in some cases acceptance of the earth's deterioration. The Zion we pursue has grass, trees, streams, oceans, wildlife, and humanity living in harmony and cooperation. It is our response to "For God so loved the world."

> c. Let the educational and community development endeavors of the church equip people of all ages to carry the ethics of Christ's peace into all arenas of life. Prepare new generations of disciples to bring fresh vision to bear on the perplexing problems of poverty, disease, war, and environmental deterioration. Their contributions will be multiplied if their hearts are focused on God's will for creation.

We are more than what we say we believe. Sadly, we have reduced faith to statements of belief, and much energy is consumed in refining, proclaiming, debating, and defending them. Yet one of the major divisive issues in Christianity lies not in theological conflict but in the polarity between *pietism* (i.e., a conviction that the church's central purpose is praise and worship) and *activism* (i.e., a conviction that the church's central purpose is personal, societal, and environmental transformation). Certainly, most Christians do not see pietism and activism as mutually exclusive expressions of faith. Nevertheless, in cultures that radically mandate the separation of church and state, religious political activism is (more often than not) silent. A faith that risks nothing is worth nothing.

The first sentence, "Let the educational and community development endeavors of the church equip people to carry the ethics of Christ's peace into all arenas of life," knits piety (e.g., worship/education) and activism (community endeavors) together equally—each serving the other. The phrase "all arenas of life" reminds us that programs and resources to activate the ethics of peace extend far beyond the church's efforts, and reminds us that we have been commissioned to be "in the forefront of those organizations and movements which are recognizing the worth of persons" (Doctrine and Covenants 151:9). As previously stated, Section 163's ecological emphasis extends this call to embrace environmental stewardship.

Paragraph 4c challenges us to "equip people of all ages" and "to prepare new generations of disciples" for the peacebuilding task. It would be easy to slip by these phrases without taking due notice of the call "to *carry the ethics* of Christ's peace" and "to bring fresh vision" to this effort. The song, "It's a Small World," has never been more true. Ironically, the shrinking of the globe has brought us closer together while at the same time moving us farther apart. Instant communication, the Internet, speedy international travel, etc., have broadened our understanding of the rich blessings of culture while confronting us with a complexity of ideologies, theologies, and lifestyles. What does it mean to "carry the ethics of Christ's peace" in a world woven with diverse cultural and religious threads where values differ?

Note that the text references "ethics," not values or beliefs. Certainly values and beliefs are important. We must continually strive to clearly articulate the principles that undergird our faith. Nevertheless, there is a difference between belief and faith. Theology, or religious belief, is faith seeking understanding. One can believe all the right things and still be unethical. Similarly, there is a difference between values and principles. Values are subjective. We decide, for the most part, what we deem valuable. Whereas I may place a high value on a computer, an iPod, or watching a hockey game, my wife may place little or no value on these. Ethical principles, however, are objective—they stand on their own strength and merit. Few would argue that *honesty, integrity, kindness, forgiveness, love, friendship,* and *sacrifice* have little or no value.

To "carry the ethics of Christ's peace," then, is to live a life that clearly demonstrates the core of Christ's ministry: love—love rooted in acts of shalom, which makes for creation's highest good; love that overrides theological persuasions whether they be liberal, conservative, Christian, or non-Christian. We wear our ethics on our sleeve, so to speak. We carry Christ's ethics with us, and they carry us. We carry them in our daily actions, reactions, and responses to people we meet and the good and not-so-good circumstances we face.

The "preparation of new generations" lays a responsibility on the present generation to not merely hand down the faith or pass on the torch, but to reinterpret the gospel in ways that are appealing and relevant to today's generation. Again, the mandate to discover new pathways is reiterated in the challenge to "to bring *fresh* vision" to bear on a hurting world.

Paragraph 4: Questions for Reflection and Discussion

1. **Discernment Exercise**: Find a quiet place. Sit silently for several minutes. Empty your mind of concerns and distracting voices. Acknowledge you are in the presence of the Holy. Read paragraph 4 **several times** aloud or silently. Do so without searching for its meaning or interpretation. Simply read it repeatedly and allow the text to **choose you**. Close the text and sit silently for a short period. What words or phrases begin to surface? With pen and pad write down whatever insights or thoughts come to mind.

2. The margins separating the affluent from the poor and dispossessed are so wide that the poor, for many, have been pushed off life's page—their faces and voices seen and heard fleetingly in magazines, newsprint, and telethons. Paragraph 4a challenges us to erase these margins. What do the sentences "Do not turn away from them. For in their welfare resides your welfare" say to you?

3. Every 3.6 seconds someone dies of poverty-related causes around the world. What are "poverty-related causes?" How does your congregation minister to the "poor, displaced, mistreated, and diseased"?

4. Ecological issues, particularly global-warming, are no longer peripheral topics. We have been instructed to be in the forefront of those who seek to heal the earth. How do you see your congregation (corporately and individually) ministering to this need? In what ways can you personally respond to the environmental counsel of Section 163?

5. "Let the educational and community development endeavors of the church equip people of all ages to carry the ethics of Christ's peace into all arenas of life." Review the statistics below. What specific actions can the church and its members take to help elevate these issues?

   - One billion adults in the world are illiterate—representing approximately 26 percent of the world's adult population.

   - Women make up two-thirds of all non-literates.

   - 98 percent of all non-literates live in developing countries.

   - 52 percent of all non-literates live in India and China.

   - Africa as a continent has a literacy rate of less than 60 percent.[16]

6. What are some ways to "prepare new generations of disciples to bring fresh vision to bear on the perplexing problems of poverty, disease, war, and environmental deterioration?"

---

[16] Source: *www.sil.org/literacy/LitFacts.htm*

Prayer of Commitment

Compassionate God,

>who weeps for the poor and wounded,

>forgive our self-absorption—our penchant to circumscribe life

>with our needs and comfort at its center.

Open our ears to the cries of the lost, the least, and the labeled.

Let the tears of others be our tears.

Let the hopes of the displaced, diseased,

>and mistreated be our hopes.

Not in word only, God—but in willful acts of love

>multiplied by your grace.

We are one with your creation, God,

>yet we have ravaged its beauty by wanton consumption.

May we heal its wounds, for its wounds are your wounds and our wounds.

Let this prayer come alive in us. Let it speak loudly.

Let us be its "amen"—the "so be it" of who we are

>and who you are calling us to be.

Reading: "A Deeper Self"

Show us, God, our deeper self.

Sister earth, brother sky, soil and soul united.

Each drop of rain, each bird's refrain…

 the very air we breathe—we are!

Wind, wave, wounded landscapes,

 creatures great and small

 groan for liberation and we hear it not at all.

Each muffled sigh, each muted cry

 are voices that we own, for they are ours

 —our deeper self, our "otherness"

 —not nature's prayer alone.

God, the music of creation plays not for us.

We are but a single note added to its song

 whose cosmic composition flows

 from eons lost and long.

One brief note, so late upon the scene,

 self-glorified, self-amplified,

 yet barely heard or seen.

Let it harmonize, not patronize,

Let it bless, not burden—heal, not hurt.

Let it join with all creation in a rhapsody of peace.

We are one. We are many.

We are the earth! Walking, talking, breathing

 —praying for release.

Reading: "Inseparable"

Speak to us of your peace, Jesus.

Not our peace: tight, limiting

—circumscribed by human wants and needs,

while creation groans and we hear it not.

We have placed ourselves far above that which we are.

From dust we come, to dust we return.

We are the earth betraying itself—

euthanizing its wonder, choking its air,

stripping its streams, insatiably obliterating

sister creatures great and small

—hell-bent to dance our dance and have it all.

Speak to us of a peace that doesn't sleep

—a peace that multiplies joys and divides sorrows

—a peace that celebrates creation

—a peace at war with separation,

for to love one is to love all,

and to wound one is to wound all.

Be a People of Compassion

8.7.8.7. D

Tune: ALL THE WAY (*Hymns of the Saints* #447)

God is weeping for creation—For its suffering need not be,
And the healing it is seeking Is alive in you and me.
"Be my hands, my feet, my blessing, You can set creation free.
Be a people of compassion—Quick to answer 'Lord, send me!'"

Hear the pleadings of the lonely, Of the hungry and diseased,
Of the poor, displaced, mistreated, Who are crying for release,
For their welfare is your welfare—Let your love for them increase.
Be a people of compassion—Be my hope, my living peace.

Let the milk of human kindness Pour its blessings on the earth,
For it shudders and is burdened When we desecrate its worth.
None stand higher than creation—It sustains us from our birth.
Be a people of compassion—Faithful stewards of God's earth.

Seek God's will for all creation, Every age can join the task.
Bear the burdens of the wounded, Lift the hopes of those downcast,
Teach and train each generation, Bring fresh vision to the task.
Be a people of compassion, Ending strife and war at last.

God Is Weeping for Creation

8.7.8.7.8.7.8

Tune: DIVINUM MYSTERIUM (*Hymns of the Saints #220*)

God is weeping for creation—For its suffering need not be,
And the healing it is seeking Is alive in you and me.
"Be my hands, my feet, my blessing, You can set creation free
Evermore and evermore!

Hear the pleadings of the lonely, The hungry and diseased,
And the poor, displaced, mistreated, Who are crying for release.
For their welfare is your welfare—Let your love for them increase
Evermore and evermore!

Let the milk of human kindness Pour its blessings on the earth,
For it shudders and is burdened When we desecrate its worth.
None stand higher than creation—It sustains us from our birth
Evermore and evermore!

Seek God's will for all creation, Every age can join the task.
Bear the burdens of the wounded, Lift the hopes of those downcast,
Teach and train each generation, Bring fresh vision to the task
Evermore and evermore!

God, Whose Heart Is Weeping

6.5.6.5. D

Tune: BJORKLAND MAJOR (*Hymns of the Saints #377*)

God, whose heart is weeping For a world in need—
God, whose heart is crying, "Set my children free,"
We can end their suffering. We can dry their tears.
We can feed the hungry. We can banish fears.

God, whose tears are flowing For creation's plight—
God, whose voice is pleading, "You can make things right,"
We can cease our feeding Endless appetites.
We can hold in balance That which gives Earth life.

God, whose hope-filled future Lives inside of you—
God, whose faith is steadfast, Seeking to renew.
We will be Love's witness And your peace pursue.
We will be your people in all we say and do.

Be Love's Living Witness

6.5.6.5. D

Tune: HERMAS (*Hymns of the Saints* #144)

God, whose heart is weeping For a world in need—
God, whose heart is crying, "Set my children free."
We will end their suffering. We will dry their tears.
We will feed the hungry. We will banish fears.

> "Be love's living witness, Be hope's hands and feet.
> Be the peace of Jesus, Blessing all you meet."

God, whose tears are flowing For creation's plight—
God, whose voice is pleading, "You can make things right,"
We will cease our feeding Endless appetites.
We will hold in balance That which gives Earth life.

> "Be loves' living witness, Be hope's hands and feet.
> Be the peace of Jesus, Blessing all you meet."

God, whose hope-filled future Lives inside of you,
God, whose faith is steadfast, Seeking to renew.
We will be Love's witness And Christ's peace pursue.
We will be your people in all we say and do.

> "Be love's living witness, Be Love's hands and feet.,
> Be the peace of Jesus, Blessing all you meet."

Notes

Paragraph 5:
Evangelistic Ministries

5 a. The Council of Twelve is urged to enthusiastically embrace its calling as apostles of the peace of Jesus Christ in all of its dimensions. The Twelve are sent into the world to lead the church's mission of restoration through relevant gospel proclamation and the establishment of signal communities of justice and peace that reflect the vision of Christ. As the apostles move out in faith and unity of purpose, freeing themselves from other duties, they will be blessed with an increased capacity for sharing Christ's message of hope and restoration for creation.

b. To accelerate the work of sharing the gospel, the Twelve and the Seventy should be closely associated in implementing wholistic evangelistic ministries. The seventy are to be the forerunners of Christ's peace, preparing the way for apostolic witness to be more readily received.

c. Procedures regarding the calling and assignments of the Presidents of Seventy and members of the Quorums of Seventy shall be developed to facilitate the maximum level of collaboration with the Council of Twelve. The Twelve, the Presidents of Seventy, and the Quorums of Seventy should spend sufficient time together to ensure a mutual understanding of evangelistic priorities and approaches.

Paragraph 5 is a departure from the paragraphs that precede it, in that it is administrative counsel regarding church leadership. Though administrative matters are heavily weighted throughout the Doctrine and Covenants, recent sections have not included organizational directives. The specificity of paragraph 5's counsel is straightforward and begs little commentary. The yoking of the Seventy with the Council of Twelve as the chief missionary arm of the church is of long standing:

> The Seventy are to act in the name of the Lord, under the direction of the Twelve, or the traveling high council, in the building up of the church.
> —Doctrine and Covenants 104:13a

> The Twelve and Seventy are traveling ministers and preachers of the gospel....The Seventy when traveling by the voice of the church, or sent by the Twelve to minister the word where the Twelve cannot go, are in the powers of their ministration apostles.
> —Doctrine and Covenants 120:3b, d (excerpts)

Likewise, the counsel for the Twelve to "free themselves from other duties" reemphasizes guidance that has been previously given:

> As the members of the Council of Twelve withdraw from detailed administration in organized areas, responsibility to carry on the work in stakes and regions will fall more heavily upon those who have been chosen for this purpose.... Thus freed from detailed administrative duties, the Council of Twelve can give more attention to their primary work of pushing the work into new fields at homes and abroad.
> —Doctrine and Covenants 148:10c–d (excerpts)

Central to the paragraph's administrative guidance is the call for *the church* to prosecute the missionary ministries of the church through "relevant proclamation" (indirectly repeating the theme "create new pathways"). The paragraph's emphasis is broader than baptizing new members—its focus is "implementing evangelistic ministries" that "establish signal communities of justice and peace that reflect the vision of Christ" and once again points to Section 163's recurring emphasis on the "restoration of creation."

Paragraph 5: Questions for Reflection and Discussion

1. **Discernment Exercise**: Find a quiet place. Sit silently for several minutes. Empty your mind of concerns and distracting voices. Acknowledge you are in the presence of the Holy. Read paragraph 5 several times aloud or silently. Do so without searching for its meaning or interpretation. Simply read it and allow the text to **choose you**. Close the text and sit silently for a short period. What words or phrases begin to surface? With pen and pad write down whatever insights or thoughts come to mind.

2. Paragraph 5 speaks of "relevant gospel proclamation." What does this term suggest to you?

3. What would you expect to find unique about a "signal community"—what would its distinguishing features be? Can a community reflect the "vision of Christ" and still entertain religious diversity that is not exclusively Christian?

4. Paragraph 5 references the need for apostles to be freed from other duties in order to increase their capacity for sharing Christ's message. How can this counsel be applied to local congregations and to your personal witness of the gospel?

5. In what specific ways can we accelerate the work of sharing the gospel?

6. Calls to the office of seventy are initiated by the Council of Presidents of Seventy in concert with the Council of Twelve Apostles. What personality characteristics and particular gifts do you associate with people called to this ministry?

7. Discuss your understanding of the phrase "forerunners of Christ's peace."

8. How do you define or characterize the term "apostolic witness"? Are there ways in which all disciples are apostolic witnesses?

9. Discuss ways your congregation can "accelerate the work of sharing the gospel."

Worship Helps: Paragraph 5

Litany: "We Shall Bless Others"

Leader: *For generations the word "peace" has dangled at the foot of a lion, lamb, and child—a symbol of sacred community. Let it come alive in you. Let it breathe anew. Let it burst forth in vibrant witness of my love and hope for creation. Many await the blessings of its grace.*

All: **We who have been so richly blessed shall bless others in your name.**

Leader: *Fields of service lay before you. You are called to make the workbench, the school desk, the kitchen and conference table extensions of my Communion table. Ordained or not ordained, you are sent forth as apostles and bearers of peace.*

All: **We, who have been so richly blessed, shall bless others in your name.**

Leader: *Free yourselves from pursuits and voices that subtly dull and hinder your witness. The work of sharing the gospel shall be accelerated as you throw off the blanket of timidity and hesitancy.*

All: **We, who have been so richly blessed, shall bless others in your name.**

Prayer of Missionary Commitment

God, let your peace breathe in us.

Let it find expression in all we say and do.

Let it prevail over our timidity,

     our reluctance to invite others to your cause.

Too often, Lord, ours is an "everyday" discipleship

     stripped clean of missionary witness.

We have immersed ourselves in tasks deemed holy

     —plans, programs, meetings.

May these necessary tasks

     no longer hold us hostage.

May they serve, not be served.

May we seize each day with new resolve

     to speak hope to the hopeless,

     love to the loveless,

     joy to the joyless.

May we, who are so richly blessed,

     bless friend and stranger

     with the living grace of your peace.

This we pray in the name of the One

     who is Our Peace,

     Christ Jesus. Amen.

Help Us to Share Your Blessings

8.7.8.7.

Tune: HOW CAN I KEEP FROM SINGING (*Hymns of the Saints #157*)

The world awaits the peace of Christ To bless each home and nation.

Let's free ourselves from busy tasks That halt its proclamation.

For we have held to lesser things And failed in love's professing.

Your grace abounds within us, Lord—Help us to share your blessings.

The world awaits communities That signal hope and peace,

That demonstrate relationships Where war and hatred cease,

Where Earth can be restored again, Where love is our confessing.

Your grace abounds within us, Lord—Help us to share your blessings.

The world awaits the dawn of hope—That day when peace shall reign

Within the hearts and souls of all Who celebrate God's name.

Release us from our timid zeal—Our witness so confining.

Your grace abounds within us, Lord—Help us to share your blessings.

Notes

Paragraph 6: Priesthood— a Sacred Covenant

6 a. Priesthood is a sacred covenant involving the highest form of stewardship of body, mind, spirit, and relationships. The priesthood shall be composed of people of humility and integrity who are willing to extend themselves in service for others and for the well-being of the faith community.

b. Truly authoritative priesthood ministry emerges from a growing capacity to bring blessing to others. Unfortunately, there are some who have chosen to view priesthood as a right of privilege or as a platform for promoting personal perspectives. Others hold priesthood as a casual aspect of their lives without regard to appropriate levels of preparation and response.

c. The expectation for priesthood to continually magnify their callings through spiritual growth, study, exemplary generosity, ethical choices, and fully accountable ministry is always present. How can the Spirit fill vessels that are unwilling to expand their capacity to receive and give according to a full measure of God's grace and truth?

d. Counsel given previously regarding the need to develop ways whereby priesthood can magnify their ministry or determine their commitment to active service remains applicable and should be more intentionally implemented. The First Presidency will provide guidelines for processes to be applied in culturally respectful ways in the various fields of the church. Fundamentally, however, the ultimate responsibility for priesthood faithfulness rests on the individual in response to the needs and expectations of the faith community.

"Priesthood is a sacred covenant involving the highest form of stewardship of body, mind, spirit, and relationships. The priesthood shall be composed of people of humility and integrity…"

The key phrase that shapes this paragraph is its first five words: "Priesthood is a sacred covenant." All else that follows is in response to that central reality. The first two sentences echo previous instruction to the church: "It is my will that my priesthood be made up of those who have an abiding faith and desire to serve me with all their hearts, in humility and with great devotion" (D. and C. 156:8a).

Much has been written and debated regarding priesthood's unique purpose. Apart from its symbolic function, which points to the numinous, priesthood is "a sacred covenant" expressed within two exclusive arenas of ministry: (1) to celebrate the sacraments, and (2) the right of presidency (leadership). In a broader context (although not specific to ordination) one might also include that this ministry is charged with calling church membership to faithfulness and to serve as exemplars. The phrase "exemplary generosity" later in the document (paragraph 6c) goes beyond financial response but embraces a generosity of spirit that spills itself freely in ministries of caring for the membership and community.

The operative word in the first sentence of paragraph 6a is the verb "involving." A quick read that casually slips over this predicate may suggest to the reader that priesthood is "the highest form of stewardship of body, mind, spirit, and relationships." That such is not the case is exemplified in the next statement's declaration that priesthood "shall be composed of people of humility and integrity" willing to serve others and "the well-being of the faith community." It could be said that the word "involving" is the pivotal concern woven throughout paragraph 6, i.e., what does truly effective, authoritative, or faithful priesthood ministry involve?

---

b. Truly authoritative priesthood ministry emerges from a growing capacity to bring blessing to others. Unfortunately, there are some who have chosen to view priesthood as a right of privilege or as a platform for promoting personal perspectives. Others hold priesthood as a casual aspect of their lives without regard to appropriate levels of preparation and response.

Authoritative priesthood ministry involves divine authority, legal authority, acknowledged authority, moral authority, and applied authority. The emphasis of paragraph 6 is primarily on moral and applied authority, caught up in such phrases as "appropriate levels of preparation and response," "continually magnify their callings," "fully accountable ministry," and "commitment to active service." Paragraph 6b minces no words—casual holding of priesthood and misuse of priesthood for personal gain are unacceptable. Similar counsel came to the church in Section 156:

> There have been priesthood members over the years, however, who have misunderstood the purpose of their calling. Succumbing to pride, some have used it for personal aggrandizement. Others, through disinterest or lack of diligence, have failed to magnify their calling or have become inactive. When this has happened, the church has experienced a loss of spiritual power, and the entire priesthood structure has been diminished.
>
> —D. and C. 156:7b–d

Priesthood authority has never been measured by whom God calls but by ministry actualized. Its value is neither greater nor less than its blessings offered and received. Many serve humbly, sacrificially, and with great devotion in the priesthood while others passively continue to carry but its name. Paragraph 6 challenges us to delve more deeply into the meaning, purpose, and accountability of priesthood, focused less on the letter of the law and more on the spirit of blessing this ministry brings. Priesthood must not be status driven. It is neither a label worn nor a title assumed—it is ministry given. Truly authoritative priesthood involves humility, integrity, preparation, spiritual growth, study, generosity, and ethical choices that are actively obvious or measurable.

---

c. The expectation for priesthood to continually magnify their callings through spiritual growth, study, exemplary generosity, ethical choices, and fully accountable ministry is always present. How can the Spirit fill vessels that are unwilling to expand their capacity to receive and give according to a full measure of God's grace and truth?

We tend to view priesthood from a realist perspective, that is, we think of priesthood as self-existent—a separate, objective reality independent of the person. For example, we may talk about priesthood being "restored," priesthood being "conferred," or "he or she holds an office in the priesthood," etc. Paragraph 6 neither denies the spiritual empowerment nor the blessings that ordination brings to those called to such ministry but leans toward a nominalist perspective of priesthood. In other words, priesthood does not enjoy independent existence but rather names unique arenas of ministry that take on reality only when ordained persons function actively in their calling and giftedness. Priesthood is not something we put on and take off. It is not initiation into a sacred society; it is not who we are but what we say and do. It is a call to specific avenues of service within a context of ministry shared by all disciples.

"How can the Spirit fill vessels that are unwilling to expand their capacity to receive and give according to a full measure of God's grace and truth?" It has been said that we give of our best and God makes up the difference. Paragraph 6c reminds us that the Holy Spirit will not do for us what we can do for ourselves. To give of one's best is to sharpen our skills, increase our knowledge, and strive for excellence. Only then is our ministry magnified.

> d. Counsel given previously regarding the need to develop ways whereby priesthood can magnify their ministry or determine their commitment to active service remains applicable and should be more intentionally implemented.

Previous counsel regarding priesthood accountability came to the church in Doctrine and Covenants sections 156 and 162:

> Therefore, where there are those who are not functioning in their priesthood, let inquiry be made by the proper administrative officers, according the provisions of the law, to determine the continuing nature of their commitment.
> —D. and C. 156:8b

> As a prophetic people you are called, under the direction of the spiritual authorities and with the common consent of the people, to discern the divine will for your own time and in the places where you serve. You live in a world with new challenges, and that world will require new forms of ministry. *The priesthood must especially respond to that challenge, and the church is admonished to prayerfully consider how calling and giftedness in the Community of Christ can best be expressed in a new time.*—D. and C. 162:2c

As a prophetic people we remain open to expanded understanding of "new forms of ministry," ordained and not ordained. Blessed by a priesthood structure that embraces multiple offices, each with a unique portfolio of responsibilities, we are challenged continually to seek ways to more effectively bless others with a fuller "measure of God's grace and truth." Are there untapped applications, modifications, and reinterpretations of priesthood ministry that await us?

Counsel to prayerfully consider how calling and giftedness are expressed undergirds Section 163's admonition regarding casualness on the part of some priesthood. If calls to priesthood responsibility are casual and

without due spiritual diligence, why would inactivity by those called be a surprise? Have we subtly and unconsciously perpetuated a system that venerates calls to the priesthood as recognition of worth, i.e., a promotion from discipleship? Will tradition prevent us from embracing fresh insights and deeper understandings of priesthood's purpose and effectiveness?

> Be respectful of tradition. Do not fail to listen attentively to the telling of the sacred story, for the story of scripture and of faith empowers and illuminates. *But neither be captive to time-bound formulas and procedures. Remember that instruction given in former years is applicable in principle and must be measured against the needs of a growing church*, in accordance with the prayerful direction of the spiritual authorities and the consent of the people.—D. and C. 161:5

"The First Presidency will provide guidelines for processes to be applied in culturally respectful ways in the various fields of the church. Fundamentally, however, the ultimate responsibility for priesthood faithfulness rests on the individual in response to the needs and expectations of the faith community."

Paragraph 6d once again mandates the First Presidency to provide specific means for priesthood to magnify their ministry and determine levels of active service. Certainly the phrase "priesthood faithfulness" has a better ring to it than "priesthood accountability" with its "letter of the law" flavor. Be that as it may, the thrust here is not punitive. The emphasis of the required guidelines should, as stated, seek to "magnify" ministerial efforts through encouragement and affirmation for those seeking to be more effective in their calling and provide incentive for those whose activity is wanting.

Paragraph 6: Questions for Reflection and Discussion

1. **Discernment Exercise**: Find a quiet place. Sit silently for several minutes. Empty your mind of concerns and distracting voices. Acknowledge you are in the presence of the Holy. Read paragraph 6 **several times** aloud or silently. Do so without searching for its meaning or interpretation. Simply read it repeatedly and allow the text to **choose you**. Close the text and sit silently for a short period. What words or phrases begin to surface? With pen and pad write down whatever insights or thoughts come to mind.

2. Priesthood are called through the spirit of revelation and wisdom. Discuss our present means of processing and approving priesthood calls. What changes, if any, would you recommend?

3. The commentator suggested that priesthood serve also as exemplars. Should priesthood be held to a higher standard of Christian lifestyle? If so, how? If not, why not?

4. Section 163 states clearly that priesthood is a "sacred covenant." Does this differ from the "sacred covenant" of discipleship?

5. Reflect on priesthood members who have had a positive and lasting influence on your life. What qualities did they exhibit? What stands out in your memory regarding the quality of their ministry? How did they magnify their calling? In contrast, have there been others, in your experience, who have been "unwilling to expand their capacity to receive and give accordingly" of their gifts of ministry? What characteristics separate these two?

6. Presently, those who are called are expected to complete three courses: (1) A course on the duties and responsibilities of the particular office to which they will be ordained; (2) Introduction to Scripture; and (3) Introduction to Ministry. Should there be prerequisites to calling and ordination, and what should these be? What courses, in addition to those mentioned, should ordinands complete?

7. We have been admonished "to prayerfully consider how calling and giftedness in the Community of Christ can best be expressed in a new time." What changes in priesthood calling, roles, and accountability would best serve our time?

8. What methods of discerning priesthood commitment and faithfulness do you think would be helpful?

9. Should calls to priesthood offices be localized, that is, be effective and authoritative only within a specific congregation or mission center; or should they be universally recognized throughout the church?

Worship Helps: Paragraph 6

Reading: Moses Moments

Reader 1: *Step back. Take a breath.* Listen carefully to the other voice—the one you prefer not to hear—the one calling you to ministry.

Reader 2: Surely, there are others, Lord. Call *them*. Send *them*.

Reader 1: *Step back. Take a breath. Listen* to the voice that says, "Slow down. It's not settled"—the voice that reminds you of your tendency to rush to judgment—to declare the verdict is in—signed, sealed, delivered. Case closed! Whenever you favor what you think you know, and what you think is right at the cost of what is right, the case is always closed. Step back. Take a breath. Listen, the voice is calling.

Reader 2: Surely, there are others, Lord. Call *them*. Send *them*.

Reader 1: *"Have you not already given all there is to give in the waters of baptism? Now is your time. I am in you and you are in me. I have no other hands but your hands, no other feet but your feet."*

Reader 2: Surely, you have the wrong person, God. I mean, who am I—and for that matter, who are you? Whom shall I say sent me? They'll never believe me. I'm not eloquent. Send someone else…and, why isn't that bush burning?

Reader 1: Life's little Moses moments come to us all. Step back. Take a breath. Listen carefully to the voice: "Slow down. It isn't settled. Trust me—there is far more to you than you think there is!

Prayer of Confession and Recommitment

God, hands have been laid upon us,

    prayers have been uttered, hymns have been sung,

    and friends and family have rejoiced in our call to ministry.

We have studied and prepared.

We have held hands of the sick, broken bread, blessed wine,

    shared your word across pulpits,

    board rooms, and lunch counters.

We have blessed and been blessed.

Now hear our confession, Lord:

For we have warmed ourselves

    at the hearth of praise and bask in light meant for you.

Idleness and apathy have called our name.

Forgive our self-indulgence. Strip away our self-sufficiency.

Restore your Spirit within us.

Let humility illumine the wonder of your call in us

    that we might, once again, be blessed to be a blessing.

In Jesus' name, we pray. Amen.

Ordination Hymn

Let the Peace of Christ Assure You

8.7.8.7.8.7

Tune: LAUDA ANIMA (*Hymns of the Saints #41*)

When God's call.to serve looms larger Than the strength you have today,
When the dark of doubt enfolds you, When the voice of fear gives sway—
Let the peace of Christ assure you And God's grace will pave the way.

When the path's unclear before you, When you don't know where to turn,
When the questions that you're asking Fail to ease your heart's concern,
Let the peace of Christ assure you That God's answer you'll discern.

Should to distant lands and places You be called to share Christ's peace
And the pain of separation Bear its weight with no release,
Let the peace of Christ assure you That God's comfort shall increase.

As these hands are laid upon you May the unction of God's grace
Bless this prayer of ordination Far beyond this time and place.
Let the peace of Christ live in you As the Spirit you embrace.

Notes

Paragraph 7: Scripture— an Indispensable Witness

7 a. Scripture is an indispensable witness to the Eternal Source of light and truth, which cannot be fully contained in any finite vessel or language. Scripture has been written and shaped by human authors through experiences of revelation and ongoing inspiration of the Holy Spirit in the midst of time and culture.

b. Scripture is not to be worshiped or idolized. Only God, the Eternal One of whom scripture testifies, is worthy of worship. God's nature, as revealed in Jesus Christ and affirmed by the Holy Spirit, provides the ultimate standard by which any portion of scripture should be interpreted and applied.

c. It is not pleasing to God when any passage of scripture is used to diminish or oppress races, genders, or classes of human beings. Much physical and emotional violence has been done to some of God's beloved children through the misuse of scripture. The church is called to confess and repent of such attitudes and practices.

d. Scripture, prophetic guidance, knowledge, and discernment in the faith community must walk hand in hand to reveal the true will of God. Follow this pathway, which is the way of the Living Christ, and you will discover more than sufficient light for the journey ahead.

"Scripture is an indispensable witness to the Eternal Source of light and truth, which cannot be fully contained in any finite vessel or language. Scripture has been written and shaped by human authors..."

The Community of Christ holds scripture in high esteem as an *indispensable witness* to light and truth. It is worth noting that paragraph 7a delineates, or at least subtly separates, scripture's role to *bear witness* of truth from the *Eternal Source* of truth. This distinction may sound like splitting hairs but it serves to remind us that scripture is not a divine product but a human product. The church does not subscribe to plenary inspiration (i.e., belief that inspired utterance spoken or transcribed is wholly complete and inerrant).

> Scripture is vital and essential to the church, but not because it is inerrant (in the sense that every detail is historically or scientifically correct). Scripture makes no such claim for itself. Rather, generations of Christians have found scripture simply to be trustworthy in keeping them anchored in revelation, in promoting faith in Christ, and in nurturing the life of discipleship. For these purposes, scripture is unfailingly reliable (2 Timothy 3:16–17).[17]

The following reflections on paragraph 7, though generally applicable to the Book of Mormon and Doctrine and Covenants, will focus primarily on our central text of scripture, the Bible. In recent years the church has referenced the New Revised Standard Version of the Bible (NRSV) in concert with Joseph Smith Jr.'s Bible

---

[17] See Community of Christ statement on scripture, "Affirmation Five"—www.CofChrist.org.

revision (i.e., the "Inspired Version") in its printed resources. The NRSV was translated from *earlier manuscripts* than were available for the translation of the Authorized (King James) version, which Joseph used to make his revisions. Again, regardless of the many versions of the Bible available (some being superior to others) none can claim inerrancy.[18]

Someone said, "The Bible is true, and some of it happened." In other words, scripture's value does not depend on historical factuality.[19] Theologian Marcus J. Borg argues that conflict about how to see and read the Bible is the single greatest issue dividing Christianity in North America today.[20] Some view the Bible through a *historical-metaphorical* lens (to see and affirm meanings beyond what the texts meant in their ancient setting[21]). Others view the Bible through a *literal-factual* lens (i.e., God said it, I believe it, that settles it). Borg maintains that biblical infallibility and biblical literalism typically go together.

> Viewing the Bible as a divine product with a divine guarantee exists in both harder and softer forms. The hard form leads to claims of biblical infallibility or inerrancy....Softer forms of literalism are willing to grant that not all of the biblical stories are to be understood in a literal-factual way...but soft literalism affirms that the really important events in the Bible happened more or less as they are described.[22]

Not only has "scripture been written and shaped by human authors"—it has been written and rewritten. Biblical scholar Bart D. Ehrman, in *"Misquoting Jesus: The Story Behind Who Changed the Bible and Why,"* chronicles the development of the Bible through a myriad of language translations, variations, and manuscripts.

> We don't have the first copies of the originals. We don't have copies of the copies of the originals. What we have are copies made later—much later. In most instances, they are copies made centuries later. And these copies all differ from one another...there are more differences among our manuscripts than there are words in the New Testament.[23]

Does this mean scripture is unreliable? Yes, if one views it through a lens of infallibility. No, if one discerns the *truth and light* it bears. Paragraph 7 is saying to us that the witness of scripture is vital, but its vitality rests on our willingness to seek to interpret it responsibly. This counsel embraces our use of all writings deemed sacramental:

> With other Christians, we affirm the Bible as the foundational scripture for the church. In addition, the Community of Christ uses the Book of Mormon and the Doctrine and Covenants as scripture. We do not use these sacred writings to replace the witness of the Bible or improve upon it.[24]

In a sense, paragraph 7 is saying that in our worship services the words "Hear the word of the Lord" sometimes spoken following the reading of a passage of scripture might well be changed to, "Hear what the Spirit is saying to the church."[25] In Borg's words, "the Spirit of God speaks through the human words of these ancient documents: The Bible is a sacrament of the sacred."[26]

Thoughts, ideas, feelings (and certainly, the Divine) cannot be captured by strings of letters woven into words or the stories they seek to spin whether they do so in paperback novels or holy writ. Our love affair with "facts" has co-opted some to secure scripture's validity in facts (quoted or contextualized) or historical events verified.

The power of sacred text is measured by its ability to reveal inspired truth regardless of who wrote what, how, where, and when. Scripture's authority is proportionate to its capacity to contain truth—and profound truth is not hostage to particular truth. The truths within our sacred books stand on their own merit. They speak for themselves. The bottom line is that revelation (in any form) is never complete unless there is a change in attitude and behavior.

---

b. Scripture is not to be worshiped or idolized. Only God, the Eternal One of whom scripture testifies, is worthy of worship. God's nature, as revealed in Jesus Christ and affirmed by the Holy Spirit, provides the ultimate standard by which any portion of scripture should be interpreted and applied.

---

[18] Joseph Smith's Bible revision is not a translation (from original biblical languages) and was not published during his lifetime. There is strong textual and historical evidence that he did not complete his work. Some passages were changed, but parallel references were not changed. A committee (appointed following the General Conference of 1886) had to decipher four varied and conflicting manuscripts in preparation for its publication.

[19] See Marcus J. Borg, *The Heart of Christianity* (New York: HarperSanFrancisco, 2003), 51

[20] Marcus J. Borg, *Reading the Bible Again for the First Time: Taking the Bible Seriously but Not Literally* (New York: HarperSanFrancisco, 2001), 4.

[21] Ibid., p. 40. Borg goes on to say, "The historical needs the metaphorical so that the text is not imprisoned in the past. The metaphorical needs the historical so that it does not become subjective fancy (p. 44).

[22] Marcus J. Borg, The Heart of Christianity), 8–9.

[23] Bart D. Ehrman, Misquoting Jesus: The Story Behind Who Changed the Bible and Why, (New York: HarperSanFrancisco, 2005), 10.

[24] See Community of Christ statement on scripture. "Affirmation 9"—*www.CofChrist.org.*

[25] Marcus J. Borg, Reading the Bible Again for the First Time, 33.

[26] Ibid., p. 33

c. It is not pleasing to God when any passage of scripture is used to diminish or oppress races, genders, or classes of human beings. Much physical and emotional violence has been done to some of God's beloved children through the misuse of scripture. The church is called to confess and repent of such attitudes and practices.

d. Scripture, prophetic guidance, knowledge, and discernment in the faith community must walk hand in hand to reveal the true will of God. Follow this pathway, which is the way of the Living Christ, and you will discover more than sufficient light for the journey ahead.

Though our church history is not rooted in Protestantism, our theological heritage *is* rooted in "the Protestant Principle." Paul Tillich championed this phrase, which in essence says we will not yield to any form of idolatry (i.e., nothing finite substitutes for the infinite).[27] Valuing scripture as the literal inerrant word of God is a form of idolatry. It is akin to placing God between the covers of a book. That which is imperfect and finite is revered as perfect and infinite. Paragraph 7b cautions that only "God, the Eternal One of whom scripture testifies, is worthy of worship."

Not all sacred writings rise to the same level of import. Few lives, if any, have been transformed by the listings of *begats* in the Hebrew Bible (the Christian "Old Testament"), or the ancestry of Jesus in the New Testament. In other words, there is *canon* (that which has authority) *within* the canon of scripture. Many of us have favorite passages (personal canon) that have served to comfort, guide, and shape our lives.

Scripture can be used and abused. Paragraph 7c admonishes against the use of scripture to "proof-text" personal agendas bent on diminishing and oppressing "races, genders, or classes of people." Tragically, scripture has been misused to condone slavery, pre-emptive war, segregation, desecration of the environment, subjugation of women, prejudice based on sexual orientation, and the list goes on.

Paul reminds us that the spirits of prophets are subject to the prophets (1 Corinthians 14:32). The saying, "A text without context is a pretext" comes into play here. The authors of scripture could not escape the context of their culture, their limitations of knowledge, or their place in history. The *holiness code* of Leviticus chapters 17–26 with its laws pertaining to clean and unclean food, purification of women after childbirth,

death penalty for adultery, etc., and texts such as "...go and smite Amalek, and utterly destroy all that they have; do not spare them, but kill both man and woman, infant and suckling, ox and sheep, camel and ass" (I Samuel 15:3 RSV) would not see many hands raised to include them in the Doctrine and Covenants as inspired counsel to today's church. Do we then simply jettison these and other disturbing verses in an effort to sanitize scripture? No, because to do so would be to strip it of its power to speak prophetically (i.e., truthfully) and graphically of the full range of the divine/human narrative that bares our vices as well as victories. Scripture must confront us with who we have been, who we are, and—most important—who we may become. Again, context is the key. Its authors neither wrote with holy pens nor foresaw their words weighted down by canonization. When we neuter scripture we rob it of its beauty as well as its rawness. To do so is to secularize the sacred and render it impotent.

I noted early in the preface to this study that not all sections of the Doctrine and Covenants were immediately canonized. Some revelations of Joseph Smith were included years following their introduction to the church. Although the Doctrine and Covenants is contemporary scripture, its counsel is also subject to culture, historical perspective, and the spirit of the prophets.

The Doctrine and Covenants contains what is *timely* (a reflection of the times) and what is *timeless* (expressions of universal truth), and we are obligated to discern such differences. For example, references to the Aaronic priesthood as being "the lesser priesthood"

---

[27] See Paul Merritt Bassette, "The Holiness Movement and the Protestant Principle" (*www.wesley.nnu.edu/wesleyan_theology/theojrnl/16-20/18-01.htm*).
Bassette writes:

"In 1948, in his book *The Protestant Era*, Paul Tillich discussed what he called the 'Protestant Principle.' Drawing on the conviction that faith must not be mere assent to doctrinal statements but must instead be radical, obedient response to the Word of God, Tillich insisted that there is at the heart of Protestantism an understanding and experience of grace in which the security apparently offered by right belief or right behavior or other religious exactitudes is shattered and we are cast upon the mercy of God and nothing else. This radical, obedient response to the Word of God was what Tillich dubbed the 'Protestant Principle.' "—3Cf. Paul Tillich, *The Protestant Era* (Chicago: University of Chicago Press, 1948).

"Negatively put, the Protestant Principle systematically forbids anything human in the place of ultimacy in the Church. No creed, no organizational structure, no person or group of persons, no custom or habit, no idea, nothing human is to be allowed supremacy....Positively put, the Protestant Principle systematically puts forward the absolute sovereignty of God."—John Dillenberger and Claude Welch, *Protestant Christianity: Interpreted Through Its Development* (New York: Charles Scribner's Sons, 1954), 313–14.

and an "appendage" are problematic but may reflect the overriding hierarchical and patriarchal milieu common to the nineteenth century. Section 20 (given April 1830, within weeks of the church's incorporation) is clear regarding the question of rebaptism. However, some question whether this text is a reflection of Joseph Smith Jr.'s conviction of priesthood authority and the need to secure exclusivity for the infant organization of the church, rather than *timeless* inspired counsel. Questions regarding rebaptism continue to resurface despite section 20. Another example where *timeliness* and *context* must be weighed in the balance is section 116. The preface to this section wisely cautions the reader that the section's statement "Be not hasty in ordaining men of the Negro race to offices in my church" should be studied against the background of the American Civil War and with the social and educational status of the American Negro of that period of time.

Scripture, then, is not meant to hold us hostage, but to free us to become God's people. This requires a willingness to have a lover's quarrel with our faith, to delve deeply into the words of inspired counsel for enlightenment. Mark said it best: "(let the reader understand)" (Mark 13:14 RSV). We cannot neatly overlay a twenty-first century template on writings written in ancient times by ancient cultures, nor can we fail to mine contemporary writings for greater meaning. The enlightenment and truth they pass on must come alive in us blessed by present contextual understandings and knowledge to which they were not privy.

Scripture is *indeed* important! Though foundational, it is not our only guide. Knowledge, prophetic guidance, and "discernment in the faith community" is the pathway we are called to walk—a journey where scripture serves as a light unto our feet, not a hammer in our hand.

Paragraph 7: Questions for Reflection and Discussion

1. **Discernment Exercise**: Find a quiet place. Sit silently for several minutes. Empty your mind of concerns and distracting voices. Acknowledge you are in the presence of the Holy. Read paragraph 7 **several times** aloud or silently. Do so without searching for its meaning or interpretation. Simply read it repeatedly and allow the text to **choose you**. Close the text and sit silently for a short period. What words or phrases begin to surface? With pen and pad write down whatever insights or thoughts come to mind.

2. The commentator states, "Profound truth is not hostage to particular truth." Stories can be containers of truth regardless if they reflect factual historical events. Films, plays, novels, songs, and children's fairy stories contain truth. Were Jesus' parables "story illustrations" he created to reveal truth or were they remembrances of actual events? Does this matter? If so, why? If not, why not?

3. What scripture texts have played an important role in your life? What are your favorite texts?

4. What role do the scriptures of the Restoration have in your life and the life of your congregation? How are they used in worship services and class settings?

5. What parts of the canon of scripture get the most attention in worship services? Which parts are neglected? Why does this happen?

6. Discuss the commentator's reference to "The Protestant Principle" with respect to scripture.

7. Section 163 admonishes the church to confess and repent of attitudes and practices wherein misuse of scripture has caused "physical and emotional violence" to some of God's children. Where have you seen violence or felt conflict due to the misuse of scripture? In what ways can the church (and its members) guard against its misuse?

8. Doctrine and Covenants 148:4 states: "Some of you have sought security in the words and phrases by which the faithful of earlier days have expressed their knowledge of me." Consider ways that your congregation can educate young and old on the importance of scripture as the voice of those who have gone before us—and to interpret that voice responsibly.

Reading: "Ink on a Page"

Ink on a page. Holy ink. Holy pages. Holy books.

Hard-cover gods filled with insight,

> wisdom, and wonder.

Proof-text permissions (Christian and non-Christian)

> that deny and destroy.

It's all there in several versions

> —birth, death, demons, and deity

> —onion-skin-thin, fueling faith and fancy.

It's a tight fit, God.

We've squeezed you into chapters and verses.

We've made you in our own image,

> put our words in your mouth

> and used them for love and war.

Open our eyes, our ears, our minds, and hearts, O God,

> to the rhythm of your Spirit,

> which beats beyond words on a page.

Free us from lethal literalism.

Let sacred texts point the way, not "be" the way.

Let them serve, not "be" served.

Let them unite, not divide.

Let them, once again, be a lamp unto our feet,

> not a hammer in our hands.

Prayer of Discernment

God, grant us eyes to see, ears to hear, and minds to discern
the words of those who have gone before us.
Let texts of holy writ speak to us,
unencumbered by our personal bias
—our penchant to divorce them
from their culture and context.
Let their deeper meanings, couched in poetry, praise,
metaphor, and narrative, stir in us new understandings
and a renewed response to your love.
May the unalterable truths of your gospel
spring forth from scripture
—enlivening our witness and guiding our steps.
Not as words that rule and are worshiped,
but as inspired expressions
of your abiding grace and counsel.
We give thanks for these books
wherein those claimed by your Spirit
have strived to unwrap its treasures.
May we, like them, seek always
to open ourselves to your Living Word.
This we pray, in Jesus name. Amen.

Eternal Source of Light and Truth

L.M.D (8.8.8.8.8.8.)

Tune: LAMB OF GOD (*Worship and Rejoice* # 503)
YE BANKS & BRAES (*Worship and Rejoice* #628)
DUANE STREET (*The Hymnal* #288)

Eternal Source of light and truth That guides the pen of holy writ,

Bless us that we might read within These wanting words of human script

The utterance of your Love's clear call—That seeks God's peace for one and all.

We'll lift Love's words from off each page That they may bless the present age.

We worship not these sacred texts Nor bend their words to serve our ends

For they are meant to bless and heal, To reconcile all souls as friends,

To raze the walls that separate, To liberate and set earth free.

We'll mine their truths responsibly In seeking God's community

Let scripture come alive in us—May we become your living words

To spell your grace in daily deeds That warm the heart with love conferred.

For scripture is a guide and stay When hand in hand it points the way

In concert with the Spirit's voice Its message lives anew each day.

Notes

Paragraph 8: A Sanctuary of Christ's Peace

8 a. The Temple is an instrument of ongoing revelation in the life of the church. Its symbolism and ministries call people to reverence in the presence of the Divine Being. Transformative encounters with the Eternal Creator and Reconciler await those who follow its spiritual pathways of healing, reconciliation, peace, strengthening of faith, and knowledge.

b. There are additional sacred ministries that will spring forth from the Temple as rivers of living water to help people soothe and resolve the brokenness and pain in their lives. Let the Temple continue to come to life as a sacred center of worship, education, community building, and discipleship preparation for all ages.

c. As these ministries come to fuller expression, receptive congregations in the areas around the Temple and throughout the world will be revived and equipped for more effective ministry. Vital to this awakening is the understanding that the Temple calls the entire church to become a sanctuary of Christ's peace, where people from all nations, ethnicities, and life circumstances can be gathered into a spiritual home without dividing walls, as a fulfillment of the vision for which Jesus Christ sacrificed his life.

Winston Churchill said that we shape our buildings and ever after they shape us. Similarly, author A. T. Robinson contends that "the church building is a prime aid, or a prime hindrance, to the building up of the Body of Christ.... And the building will always win."[28] If Churchill and Robinson are correct, the design and symbolism of the Temple will have a profound impact on the nature and mission of the church.

A design that spirals outward, sending its participants and ministries beyond its walls, empowered to bless creation, is a symbol that (in Paul Tillich's words) participates "in the reality of that for which it stands." Tillich declared that a "religious symbol can be a true symbol only if it participates in the power of the divine to which it points."[29] Accordingly, the Temple is more than an architectural marvel of swirling stone, steel, and glass; it is "an instrument of ongoing revelation" and transformation. President Emeritus Wallace B. Smith captured the essence of the Temple's revelatory function in the following statement:

> There is a longing in the soul of every human being for a clearer understanding of the mystery and meaning of life and that as persons have sought for understandings in the realm of religious experiences, they have been led to identify and even enshrine places where they have felt the presence of the numinous and which has helped them comprehend a bit more of the mystery which is our life—and our relatedness to the Creative Force which not only brought into being, but sustains it from day to day. We have said we believe the Temple in Independence will be such a place.[30]

---

[28] A. T. Robinson, *Making the Building Serve Liturgy*, ed. Gilbert Cope (London: A.R. Mowbray, 1962), 5.
[29] Paul Tillich, *Systematic Theology*, 3 vols. (Chicago: University of Chicago Press, 1951), Vol. 1: 229.
[30] Wallace B. Smith, as quoted in TL 100 The Temple, ed. Lyman F. Edwards (Independence, Missouri: Community of Christ, 1989), 38.

The phrase "*ongoing* revelation" in paragraph 8a lies at the heart of what it means to be a prophetic people—a people willing to be surprised and to explore that which lies beyond the horizon. The Temple bears witness of such a people, having been constructed debt free before its specific use and function were known ("It is also to be noted that the full and complete use of the temple is yet to be revealed."—D. and C., Section 149:6). Dr. J. H. Oldham writes, "There are some things in life, and they may be the most important things, that we cannot know by research or reflection, but only by committing ourselves. We must dare in order to know." [31]

Though the Temple stands as a fixed monumental edifice, the definition and redefinition of its ministries of "healing, reconciliation, peace, strengthening of faith, and knowledge" are not fixed, but continue to spring forth.

---

b. There are additional sacred ministries that will spring forth from the Temple as rivers of living water to help people soothe and resolve the brokenness and pain in their lives. Let the Temple continue to come to life as a sacred center of worship, education, community building, and discipleship preparation for all ages.

The Temple's unfolding spiral is symbolic of an unfolding faith. Likewise, its ministries continue to unfold. The specificity of the "additional sacred ministries" referenced in 8b is not spelled out. The poetic language of the paragraph characterizes them as "springing forth as rivers of living water"—a constant current of new ministerial initiatives flowing from a willingness to go beyond traditional expectations. Once again, the metaphor "pathway" comes to the fore, encouraging a readiness to dare the unexplored. The phrase "springing forth" suggests that we may be surprised by the revelatory impulse and nature of these ministries.

"Let the Temple continue to come to life" echoes, once again, the fluidity of Temple ministries. This will *always* be the case. The aliveness of the Temple will forever be commensurate with the needs of every given age. The test for every sanctuary, every sacred space, every worship and educational activity, is praxis! The Temple is called through its various ministries to transform the dining room table, the office desk, and the workbench into extensions of the Communion table. Temple worship, education, training, and ministries are not solely for the sake of those who gather within its walls, but are also for the sake of those who may never enter its doors.

Its ministries are to flow outward to "help people soothe and resolve the brokenness and pain." The Temple is not God's gift to the Community of Christ; it is a gift to enhance *life itself* wherever its influence extends.

---

c. As these ministries come to fuller expression, receptive congregations in the areas around the Temple and throughout the world will be revived and equipped for more effective ministry.

Paragraph 8c reminds us that "*receptive* congregations in areas around the Temple and throughout the world will be *revived* and equipped for effective ministry." Thus the effectiveness of the Temple's ministry will be proportionate to receptivity—to our willingness to receive and appropriate its blessings. We must be open to and take full advantage of its ministries of revival.

We need revival. In recent years, the church in North America has struggled financially and lagged in growth and expansion. Apart from Pentecostal images the word "revival" elicits, its root meaning is "to activate, to set in motion, take up again, to renew."

Many people are searching for spiritual renewal—a discovery of authenticity. The prodigal son experienced revival slopping pigs—"he came to himself"—a revival of his true, *authentic* self. Zacchaeus experienced revival across the supper table. Peter's revival happened on a rooftop, arguing with God on what to eat and not eat, and Mary's, at the feet of a supposed gardener at the tomb. Elijah experienced revival in a cave, Joseph Smith in a grove, the Emmaus travelers while breaking bread, Paul on the dusty road to Damascus, and Lydia on the banks of a river near Philippi.

Albeit the range and venues for revival are myriad, paragraph 8, in a sense, calls for a revival of the Temple itself as an instrument of spiritual awakening. The time has come for it to expand its ministries in fresh new ways to bless the community where it resides and the greater global community it serves. The Temple is called to play a significant role in "awakening" church and community to new life.

"Vital to this awakening is the understanding that the Temple calls the entire church to become a sanctuary of Christ's peace,"

Our call to be sanctuaries of Christ's peace extends well beyond stained-glass windows and pews. It is a call

---

[31] Dr. J. H. Oldham, *Life Is Commitment* (New York: Harper & Brothers, 1952).

to be a catalyst of peace in the workplace, the school-yard, the board room, the athletic field—as far and wide as our arena of influence extends. It is a call to extend "sacred space" to all whom we meet and greet. It is a call to become *living sanctuaries* in the midst of all life's inequities, ambiguities, and sudden startling joys.

All enduring religions recognize sacred space. Community of Christ theology maintains that all things are spiritual, that is, the universe is undivided and essentially sacred. This suggests that any fence between the sacred and secular is of our own making. Consequently we find ourselves dancing back and forth from one side to the other. Sanctuary is more than a sacred place—it is a sacred condition, process, and relationship—a ministry rooted in compassionate care that provides a safe harbor from life's stormy seas and embraces all creation as gift. We must continually examine our own dance between the sacred and the secular—to honestly evaluate our personal strengths and weaknesses. It tells us that the space and place for effective ministry is as broad or narrow as mutual giving and receiving will permit.

"…where people from all nations, ethnicities, and life circumstances can be gathered into a spiritual home without dividing walls, as a fulfillment of the vision for which Jesus Christ sacrificed his life."

God's love is a circle without a circumference. No one is on the outside looking in. Everyone is accepted. Unfortunately, some have not found their place within that circle. Many wounded souls are in search of hope, solace, and sanctuary. Their search is not primarily for places of sanctuary (important as these are) but for a loving community where acceptance and sanctuary rule—where the ministry of Christ is embodied and specifically expressed in affirming and transformative relationships. Paragraph 8 is a declaration that the overarching purpose of Temple ministries is to be instrumental in transforming Zionic dreams into reality—not simply in the physical shadow of its swirling spire, but wherever "people of all nations, ethnicities, and life circumstances" seek a spiritual home. A spiritual home, where Zion (the peaceable kingdom) becomes enfleshed by a lively awareness that we are one and that nothing

separates us from God's unconditional love. Eugene Peterson's Bible version, The Message, translates Romans 8:39 with these words:

> **Nothing living or dead, angelic or demonic, today or tomorrow, high or low, thinkable or unthinkable—absolutely nothing can get between us and God's love because of the way that Jesus our Master has embraced us.**

Love does not dictate sameness. It does not demand agreement. Ultimately, love makes no demands. It cannot. It embraces the diversity of creation and celebrates the blessings of unity found in the One who causes all to be. Love says, "If we cannot be on the same page, can we be on different pages in the same book? If we cannot be in the same book, can we be on the same shelf or in the same section in the same library? And, if not the same book, same section, or same library, can we at *least* celebrate that we have been *penned into creation* by the *same* Author?"

The root, then, of "becoming a sanctuary of Christ's peace" is recognition of our one-ness! Despite our individuality we are inexplicably connected. When others cry, we taste salt. Compassion arises from a mystery unexplained, yet intuitively understood, that "I am for you, because you *are me* and I *am you*." Though we cannot experience the unique pain or joy of another, we are fellow citizens of life's triumphs and tragedies. The call to be a sanctuary of Christ's peace is a call to honor spiritual journeys and religious persuasions whose paths of peace, though different from ours, are devoted to the worth of persons and who seek joy, hope, love, justice, and sacred community. It is a call to tear down walls of division and expand beyond measure a spirituality of hospitality that invites all to share God's love.

> *Something there is that doesn't love a wall,*
> *That sends the frozen-ground-swell under it*
> *And spills the upper boulders in the sun,*
> *And makes gaps even two can pass abreast.*
> —Robert Frost

As *living sanctuaries of Christ's peace*, we are called to welcome all who abide within the circle of God's love—a circle without a circumference—where all life is sacramental.

Paragraph 8: Questions for Reflection and Discussion

1. **Discernment Exercise**: Find a quiet place. Sit silently for several minutes. Empty your mind of concerns and distracting voices. Acknowledge you are in the presence of the Holy. Read paragraph 8 **several times** aloud or silently. Do so without searching for its meaning or interpretation. Simply read it repeatedly and allow the text to **choose you**. Close the text and sit silently for a short period. What words or phrases begin to surface? With pen and pad write down whatever insights or thoughts come to mind.

2. If you have visited the Temple in Independence, reflect on that experience and share with others in group discussion. How has your experience with the Temple affected your response to God's call in your life? If you have not visited the Temple, what impact has reading about it, and hearing stories about those who have visited it, had on your life?

3. When the Temple was completed, its ministries were initially focused in six centers of emphasis. Although these specific centers are no longer designated as such, the ministries described to each are ongoing:

   - The Temple Peace Center (Conflict Management/National and International Peace/Environmental Welfare)

   - The Temple Worship Center (Healing of the Spirit/Strengthening of Faith/Spiritual Awakening)

   - The Temple Missionary Center (Fostering Church Outreach/Redeeming Agent/Preparation of Witness)

   - The Temple Service Center (Support for Programming in Temple Centers/Recruitment and Training of Volunteers/Servant Ministries)

   - The Temple School (Leadership Training/Academic Exploration/Self-Realization)

   - The Temple Abundant Life Center (Reconciliation in Primary Relations/Inner Peace/Wholeness of Body, Mind, and Spirit)

   Section 163 states that "additional sacred ministries" will spring forth from the Temple. Reflect on what these might be.

4. The Temple is not a gift to the Community of Christ, but a gift to the world. Reflect on how its ministries locally and globally might be enhanced to serve all peoples.

5. Section 163 states that "the Temple calls the entire church to become a sanctuary of Christ's peace." Consider how your congregation functions as a sanctuary of Christ's peace. What is required of us as individuals to become living sanctuaries of peace?

Reading: "Each a Sanctuary"

Faith's pebble drops on the surface of life

> erupting, disrupting, rippling in concentric circles

> ever outward beyond sight and sound 'til no one knows

> from whence or where these waves of hope abound.

No spire to point to—no shadow of the cross,

> no shining steel and stone.

Far, far away a Temple stands.

Peace pointing upward, spinning skyward,

> sparkling in the sun.

More than silent sanctuary, its voice has many tongues.

It speaks to all in sunlight

> —it whispers in the night

> —its voice is never muted

> —its beacon burning bright.

Living, breathing, walking, talking

> —it comes alive in us.

No swirling spire, no shadow of the cross,

> no shining steel and stone

> —just a helping hand, a word of hope,

> a listening ear, a touch, a smile,

> a light to guide the way.

Each soul's a living sanctuary,

> —a place of hope and healing

> —a place of trust and peace

> —a place of safe acceptance

> —a love that will not cease.

Rippling ever outward, encircling lives afar,

> faith's pebble drops and spreads release

> from whence God's blessings come.

Prayer: "Sanctuaries of Peace"

Whirling, swirling skyward
    —here in this sacred space we sense your Spirit, God
    —not because other places where we walk, talk,
       and live out our daily lives are less sacred.
Every sanctuary large or small, humble or ornate
    —every living room, field, forest, mountain stream
       dedicated to your praise and peace
       awakens us to your presence.
We come expectant.
We come in search of you, of ourselves,
    of those we know and do not know
    who need to be blessed and to be your blessing.
How many feet have journeyed
    this Worshiper's Path, God?
How many faces, races, friends, families, strangers?
Heads bowed in silence.
Hearts filled with hope and anticipation.
Upward. Inward. Slowly, reflectively,
    winding their way into spiraling space.
Bringing you here, meeting you here
    —taking you with them, God.
Opening themselves, once again,
    to your ever-abiding presence at all corners of life.
And somehow awakening to the wonder that they too
    are your temple
    —each a living, loving sanctuary of peace,
    reconciliation, and healing of the spirit.
May this shining symbol escape its footings and foundation.
May it wander far and wide in crepe soles,
    sandals, high-heels, bare feet, and sneakers
    —its walls wrapped in suits, saris,
    shirts, and sundresses.
Let its face be a rainbow of cultures,
    young and old, weak and strong
    —each a living sanctuary of Christ's peace.
And may those who never enter its doors, become its doors,
    welcoming all they meet with the
    gift of grace and holy acceptance.

In Jesus name, amen.

God's Temple Comes Alive in Us

9.8.9.8

Tune: SPIRITUS VITAE (*Worship and Rejoice* # 328)
BEGINNINGS (*Worship and Rejoice* # 355)
ST. CLEMENT (*Worship and Rejoice* #107)

Can steel and stone and swirling spire That's planted in some distant place

Become God's blessing to all nations—The lost, the labeled and displaced?

Can they who never see its shadow Find solace in such sacred space?

Can ministries of living water Flow far beyond its resting place?

God's Temple comes alive in us—In every nation, tribe, and home.

It lives and breathes in every soul That seeks the peace of Jesus Christ.

Notes

Paragraph 9: Generosity Flows from Compassionate Hearts

9. Faithful disciples respond to an increasing awareness of the abundant generosity of God by sharing according to the desires of their hearts; not by commandment or constraint. Break free of the shackles of conventional culture that mainly promote self-serving interests. Give generously according to your true capacity. Eternal joy and peace await those who grow in the grace of generosity that flows from compassionate hearts without thought of return. Could it be otherwise in the domain of God, who eternally gives all for the sake of creation?

There are those who give with joy,
and that joy is their reward.
And there are those who give with pain,
and that pain is their baptism,
And there are those who give and know
not pain in giving, nor do they seek joy,
nor give with mindfulness of virtue;

They give as in yonder valley the myrtle
Breathes its fragrance into space.
Through the hand of such as these
God speaks, and from behind their eyes
He smiles upon the earth.

—*Kahlil Gibran*[32]

It has been said that the real work of stewardship is to help us grow spiritually. The 2002 World Conference saw the Presiding Bishopric introduce, under the banner "Honor God's Call to Tithe," an expanded interpretation of stewardship. The measure of one's financial stewardship took on new dimensions. All contributions supporting local congregations, World Church, or charitable agencies, etc., were defined as tithing. In a very real sense the thrust of stewardship shifted from accountability to *generosity*. The principle of tithing was by no means abandoned; instead, a renewed emphasis was placed on one's desire to share rather than calculating what one was obligated to give. In many ways this freed financial giving from the shackles of requirement, thus enlivening the work of stewardship to help us grow spiritually. This new interpretation was in direct response to previous counsel given to the church:

> **The Presiding Bishop and his counselors are encouraged to continue to seek ways of effecting a greater understanding of the meaning of the stewardship of temporalities as a response to my grace and love so that the understanding of the principle may stir the hearts of the people as never before. Redefinition of terms within the basic law of temporalities, for clarification and to meet the needs of a growing church, is in harmony with my will.**
> **—Doctrine and Covenants 154:5a–b**

Generous financial response begins with a desire to meet our obligations. It begins there, but is not content to reside there. Generosity always wants to do more! Rilke says in one of his poems to God, "We grasp you only by acting."[33] Paragraph 9 knits the act of giving to an increased *awareness of the abundant generosity*

---

[32] Kahlil Gibran, *The Prophet* (New York: Alfred A Knopf, 1973), 20.
[33] As quoted by Frederic and Mary Ann Brussat, *Spiritual Literacy: Reading the Sacred in Everyday Life* (New York: Scribner, 1996), 309.

of God. We are moved to share according to the desires of our hearts—"not by commandment or constraint." Such sharing is an act of unrestrained compassion—a recklessly righteous response quickened by a deeper grasp of God's abundant grace in our lives. There is little compassion in a law that is followed only to the letter and not by its spirit. We "break free of the shackles of conventional culture that mainly promote self-serving interests" when sharing is motivated by joy. Instead of asking, "How much tithing do I owe?" the compassionate heart asks, "How much tithing can I hope to share?"

How can we share more? Through principles of good money management. The *ten-ten-eighty principle* has proved to be an effective guideline: Ten percent of income for mission and community tithes, ten percent of income for savings, eighty percent of income for living expenses. It is suggested that the portion given to the church be *equally divided* between the local congregation and the World Church. The Presiding Bishopric makes the following recommendations:

> Agency is one of the generous gifts God gives to us. Agency is our ability to choose freely how we respond to God's infinite love and grace. Using our agency wisely allows us to manage our time, giftedness, and resources to benefit our personal, family, congregational, and community life. More specifically, our stewardship of financial resources defines the extent we can generously share, wisely save, and responsibly spend. The following six principles of A Disciple's Generous Response guide us in living out our stewardship of resources:
>
> 1. A disciple practices generosity as a spiritual discipline in response to God's grace and love.
> 2. A disciple is faithful in response to Christ's ministry.
> 3. A disciple's financial response, while unique to individual circumstances, expresses love of God, neighbor, creation, and oneself.
> 4. A disciple shares generously through tithing so that others may experience God's generosity.
> 5. A disciple saves wisely in order to create a better tomorrow for self, family, the church's mission, and the world.
> 6. A disciple spends responsibly as a commitment to live in health and harmony with God and the world.

Sharing's governing spirit, then, is not formulas but thankfulness. Rich or poor, we yearn to give to the One who has given all to us! Whether our tithe is two mites or two million—it is given with a joyful heart, saddened only by our inability to give more. Sharing is part of who we are. Bradley G. Call, in an article in *Journal of Stewardship*, suggests that generosity is part of our natural being:

> The English word [generous] comes most directly from the Latin *generosus* ("of noble birth, excellent, magnanimous") which in turn comes from the Latin *genus* ("birth, race, kind"). Going back further, the Latin words derive from the Greek root *geno-*, meaning "to become, to happen, to be." This is the root of the word "genesis" [which] means "beginnings." Put all this together and you can see that the idea of generous giving has something to do with our very being….Generous giving flows not from a demand placed on us, but from the core of our being. To be *other than* a giver not only makes us ungenerous, but denies part of our natural being.[34]

Sharing generously according to our true capacity is of course more than a monetary response—it is the sharing of one's total self (time, talent, *and* treasure). Paragraph 9 reminds us that it could not be "otherwise in the domain of God, who eternally gives all for the sake of creation."

> We all have, without exception, a very deep longing to give—to give to the earth, to give to others, to give to society, to work, to love, to care for this earth…. And there's a tremendous sorrow for a human being who doesn't find a way to give. One of the worst of human sufferings is not to find a way to love, or a place to work and give of your heart and your being.[35]

> *Living is the art of loving.*
> *Loving is the art of caring.*
> *Caring is the art of sharing.*
> *Sharing is the art of living.*
> —*Author unknown*

---

[34] Bradley G. Call, "Generous Giving," *Journal of Stewardship* 46, eds. Ronald E. Vallet and Rose Marie Vallet (Ecumenical Center for Stewardship Studies, printed in Canada, 1994): 55–57.

[35] Jack Kornfield in "Roots of Buddhist Pyschology," as quoted in *Spiritual Literacy,* eds. Frederic and Mary Ann Brussat, 327.

Paragraph 9: Questions for Reflection and Discussion

1. **Discernment Exercise**: Find a quiet place. Sit silently for several minutes. Empty your mind of concerns and distracting voices. Acknowledge you are in the presence of the Holy. Read paragraph 9 **several times** aloud or silently. Do so without searching for its meaning or interpretation. Simply read it repeatedly and allow the text to **choose you**. Close the text and sit silently for a short period. What words or phrases begin to surface? With pen and pad write down whatever insights or thoughts come to mind.

2. What was your response to the church's reinterpretation of stewardship, which includes all contributions (local congregation and World Church offerings plus all charitable donations) as tithing?

3. We have not abandoned the principle of tithes coming from one's increase, but generosity ("sharing according to the desires of your hearts, not by commandment or constraint") in essence trumps giving determined by a specific formula or calculation. How has this redefinition changed your giving pattern?

4. An old familiar saying tells us, "Charity begins at home." Is this one of the "shackles of conventional culture that promotes self-serving interests?" Stewardship guidelines recommend that contributions to church be equally divided between local congregational ministries and World Church ministries. Reflect on your personal giving pattern and that of your congregation. Discuss ways we can free ourselves to share generously with all those in need.

Worship Helps: Paragraph 9[36]

Reading: "Each Penny Is Alive"

Reader One: Each dollar, each dime, each penny dropped on the offering plate is *alive*. Checks tucked inside offering envelopes are *alive*. They are a "living sacrifice." The money we give to God's cause is more than a symbol of who we are; it represents hours spent in labor that can never be reclaimed—little pieces of ourselves spent at the workplace—whether that be at the office or at home, cutting the grass for an allowance, or enclosed in the tight security of a piggy bank.

Reader Two: Whenever we give our money we give something of ourselves. The ministries and services of the church, then, are fueled by our willingness to give freely in response to One whose consistent giving is alive in the world around us and within us. Join me this morning. Place "yourself" on the offering plate—there's room enough for all of us.

---

[36] The reading and prayers for this paragraph were written by the author and previously published in *Year A Worship Resources: Passionate for Peace*, eds. Jane M. Gardner and Peter A. Judd (Independence, MO., Herald House, 2007).

Disciples' Generous Response Prayer

We thank you, God,

    that we have been awakened by your grace.

Let us rub the sleep from our eyes

    that we might once more drink in

    the wonder of your creation of which we are a part.

Bless us beyond the meager gifts we give.

Let us be constantly amazed by your love,

    and may we amaze others with its wonder. Amen.

Disciples' Generous Response Prayer

May we, O God, freely offer our gifts

    of time, talent, and treasure,

    not counting the cost.

May we not portion them,

    divide or weigh them,

    but simply give them.

Let us rejoice as we "give thee but thine own"

    —pressed down, shaken together, and overflowing.

Thank you for making our meager gifts possible.

Bless them as you have blessed us

    so that others might be blessed. Amen.

Can We Calculate Our Giving?

8.7.8.7.D.

Tune: NETTLETON (*Hymns of the Saints* # 31)

Can we calculate our giving, Placing limits on our praise

When the blessings we are given Multiply and grace our days?

Let us share from life's abundance. God provides enough to spare—

Shaken down and pressed together, Overflowing everywhere.

Great or small the treasure offered, Each is equal in God's sight;

Fragrance poured from alabaster Valued as a widow's mite.

Bless our giving and receiving. Rich or poor can do their part—

Giving for the sake of giving, Flowing from a gen'rous heart.

God's community is living Far beyond our walls of faith.

Every tithe that serves creation Will be valued in its place.

Be it home or global mission, Any cause that strengthens worth

Will be honored in our giving As a blessing for God's earth.

Take the meager gifts we offer. Wrap them in abundant grace

So that they who shall receive them Look past us and see God's face.

May the object of our giving Strip itself of rules that bind

'Til the measure of our sharing Spills beyond what law confines.[37]

[37] Text: Danny A. Belrose, *Wave Offerings* (Independence, MO., Herald Publishing House, 2005), 25.

I See in Them Christ's Face Divine

8.8.8.8.8.8.8.8.

Tune: LAMB OF GOD (*Worship and Rejoice # 503*)
YE BANKS & BRAES (*Worship and Rejoice #628*)

When I can ache with hunger pangs For those whose bowls are washed with tears

And thirst to quench the driest tongue And visit those who live in fear,

And hold the hands of captive souls Who sit alone when death is near,

I see in them Christ's face divine And hope they see his face in mine.

When I can fill a stranger's need With friendship's hand and plant hope's seed,

Which bears love's fruit and brings relief To heavy hearts weighed downwith grief,

And share Christ's peace, which brings release From burdens born by hurt's increase,

I see in them Christ's face divine And hope they see his face in mine.

When I can share another's pain And bring to birth their joy again

With loving deeds that break each chain That binds their wounded heart's refrain.

When I esteem each soul on earth As blessed by God with priceless worth,

I see in them Christ's face divine And hope they see his face in mine.

When I can hear God's many names In whirling dance and candle flames,

In incense prayed and prayer mats laid, In songs and psalms and Wailing Wall,

When I can hear in one and all Of every sacred book God's call

I'll see in life Love's face divine And hope it sees Love's face in mine.

I See in Them Christ's Face Divine (Alternate Version)

(The hymn's verses can also be used singly as a prayer response.)

8.8.8.8

Tunes: HESPERUS (*Hymns of the Saints* #348)
BROOKSFIELD (*HS* #418)
CANNONBURY (*HS* #412)
MENDOR (*HS* #432)

When I can ache with hunger pangs For those whose bowls are washed with tears,

I see in them Christ's face divine And hope they see his face in mine.

When I can quench the driest thirst And visit those who live in fear,

I see in them Christ's face divine And hope they see his face in mine.

When I can hold each captive's hand Who sits alone when death is near,

I see in them Christ's face divine And hope they see his face in mine.

For every treasured soul's divine And every heart's the same as mine,

And every deed of love defines The face of Christ in yours and mine.

Notes

Paragraph 10: Be Vulnerable to Divine Grace

10 a. Collectively and individually, you are loved with an everlasting love that delights in each faithful step taken. God yearns to draw you close so that wounds may be healed, emptiness filled, and hope strengthened.

b. Do not turn away in pride, fear, or guilt from the One who seeks only the best for you and your loved ones. Come before your Eternal Creator with open minds and hearts and discover the blessings of the gospel anew. Be vulnerable to divine grace.

The first sentence of paragraph 10 is reminiscent of Jeremiah 31:3 "I have loved you with an everlasting love; therefore with loving kindness have I drawn you." Everlasting love, by definition, is endless and is not subject to withdrawal. There are no conditions by which it will cease. The Hebrew word *owlam* (translated as "everlasting") means: continuous existence, perpetual, everlasting, indefinite or unending future, eternity. There are more than 170 verses that describe God's love as being "steadfast" (meaning firmly fixed in place, immovable, not subject to change—firm in belief, determination, or adherence).

We are loved "collectively and individually" regardless of our response to God's love. This is a high hurdle for some people to leap. Grace has no strings attached. The everlasting love referenced in paragraph 10 is noncontingent. It is unconditional, uncalculated, uncompromised, groundless. God's love is always seeking

yet never requiring. Love, then, is not something that God does—love is something that God *is*.

God "delights in each faithful step taken" on the path of discipleship; nevertheless, faith's journey is not all sweetness and light: "The path will not always be easy, the choices will not always be clear" (Doctrine and Covenants 161:7). Paragraph 10 assures us that "God yearns to draw you close so that wounds may be healed, emptiness filled, and hope strengthened."

The phrase "God *yearns* to draw you close" is significant, and prefigures the concluding sentence of paragraph 10, "Be vulnerable to divine grace." God's everlasting love continually reaches out to us; nevertheless, God will not impose divine love upon us. The choice to receive and respond to such love is of our choosing.

b. Do not turn away in pride, fear, or guilt from the One who seeks only the best for you and your loved ones. Come before your Eternal Creator with open minds and hearts and discover the blessings of the gospel anew.

Whenever pride, fear, or guilt separates us from God it separates us from ourselves, others, and creation itself. This is not to suggest that pride, fear, or guilt are to be denied—they have their healthy aspects. To delight in deeds accomplished and gifts bestowed; to fear what is threatening and destructive; or to come to a lively awareness of one's own short-comings blessed by a spirit of reconciliation and forgiveness are positive steps on the path of discipleship. Paragraph 10b, however, is a clear declaration that we must not permit either self-aggrandizement or its opposite (feelings of unworthiness) to turn us away from "the One who seeks only the best for [us] and [our] loved ones."

God is always bigger than our best understandings. The invitation and promise to "Come before your Eternal Creator with open minds and hearts and discover the blessing of the gospel anew" is written deeply into the constitution of the Restoration movement. Apostle Gene Austin consistently emphasized that our faith community was "a movement"—a people always on a journey of discovery and rediscovery.

A rabbi once said, "The essence of spiritual maturity is the refusal to shut doors." When theological viewpoints become hardened, defensive, brittle, and closed, the sharing and expanding of faith (the *give* and *take* of ideas) becomes "give and *no take.*" The resulting price tag of such dogmatism is a divided faith, silently and sometimes not so silently at war with itself—a cleavage of the Christian family into separate camps ironically sharing the same potluck dinners but little else.

Paragraph 10b calls us to be an "open door" people—a people with open minds and *hearts.* Whether through subtle, perhaps unconscious, discrimination, there are occasions when we are less accepting of others. We turn a blind eye and deaf ear to those whose lifestyles, beliefs, and cultural perspectives are foreign to us. Sometimes what we criticize in others is what we dislike about ourselves—a litany of our own weaknesses safely projected onto someone else. Paragraph 10 is a call to soften our hearts, to open them to healthy self-love and the love of others—to listen rather than just hear, to support rather than discourage, to assist rather than hinder, to celebrate the *oneness* of the human family and the glory of God's creation.

An "open door" people refuse to marginalize others because their faith perspectives differ. It's really a matter of refusing to shut doors. Theological labels can get in the way. Whether one's theological leanings are conservative or liberal is less important than whether one's mind is *open* or *closed.* Liberals and conservatives can be equally unyielding. Both extremes can hold so tenaciously to what was and is that they are unable to embrace the sunlight of what could be. People who open doors are enticed by cracks of sunlight and the promise of fresh air.

As referenced previously in this study, the heart of openness is *exploration.* Openness doesn't mean we must drop everything near and dear. Its mantra is not "anything goes." Sound theological exploration does not embrace every wispy wind of doctrine or cutting-edge philosophical perspective. We must not abandon tried and true universals—the ethical imperatives that hold us firmly to the ground of being. On the other hand, we cannot hold on to everything. We can no longer serve what does not serve the greater good. In effect, the doors of inadequate and unhealthy theological perspectives *swing shut themselves* in the wake of enlightenment.

"Be vulnerable to divine grace."

Today *vulnerability* has assumed center stage. The events of September 11, 2001, are seared in memory. A land and a people heretofore seemingly invulnerable to the bloodbath of terrorism tragically experienced in lands afar were suddenly thrust over the edge of tranquility into the midnight of confusion and despair. The aftermath of this event has been far reaching and continues to shape our lives. Its effects have spilled well beyond North America as political leaders of every stripe around the globe campaign on promises of safety and security for their people.

Ironically, our security ultimately depends on our willingness to *be vulnerable*—to be willing to put down our arms, tear down walls that separate us, and learn to live together in peace. This statement, to some people, may ring a deafening note of naïveté considering the complex and divisive religious and geopolitical issues we face—but it is the very note that the gospel sounds. There is a better way than violence. There is a better way than political machinations. There is a better way than power, might, and force. The gospel calls for peace, and peace requires trust *and* vulnerability.

We do violence to ourselves and the realization of such peace whenever and wherever we put up defenses against God's love—and this is at the heart of Section 163's counsel to be vulnerable to divine grace. It is when we rely solely on our own strength and devices to achieve peace (personal and global) that we are at our weakest. Said another way, the realization of God's kingdom on earth (Zion) is humanly impossible, but it *is* divinely possible. We must be willing to be defenseless to God's grace.

Why would anyone resist God's grace? Primarily because grace is a disquieting concept—it flies in the face of what we think is fair—our "*this* in exchange for *that*" mindset. There is no *this* for *that* with grace; there is just "this": God's everlasting love, freely given. The gospel is not a transaction. It is not realized by exchange or barter; it is not a business deal or a contract. Fundamentally, it requires giving up what we think we deserve—a willingness to *turn away* from ulterior motives and agendas. Fred Craddock writes: "What is demanded of disciples is that in the network of many loyalties in which all of us live, the claim of Christ and the gospel not only takes precedence but, in fact, redefines the others. This can and will necessarily involve some detaching, some turning away."[38]

The God of Christian assurance is not a celestial scorekeeper, but a loving parent whose love is assured regardless of what we have done or left undone—a parent who believes in us more than we believe in ourselves. Rev. Dr. Maurice Boyd illustrates God's assurance this way:

> Suppose I were to say to you, "Well, I know my wife loves me because in great kindness she constantly assures me of her love…that assurance is not in me, it's in her. It is not something of which I can boast, it is something for which I am thankful. It is not something I have accomplished, but something which she has bestowed. It doesn't lead to arrogance but to humility. It is not anything I have achieved, but something I have received.[39]

Ultimately, we are at odds with grace because receiving grace results in *surrender*—and we are not a people who surrender easily.

> Surrendering the old self to make way for the new is not easy; it requires relinquishing our power, our expectations, and our independence to make way for humility, guidance, awareness, consciousness, grace, and simplicity. Although we are sometimes forced to surrender through suffering and illness, conscious surrender for the greater good can be a celebration of belonging to God. To live in a state of surrender is to let go of our concept of time, of form, or a beginning, middle, and end of the course of life and to live solely in the present.[40]

Grace calls us to surrender the pretense that we are at the center of life—the delusion that we are in charge and control of that which spins around us and serves us. It is a matter of surrendering or letting go of subtle forms of self-idolatry. It should be noted that receiving God's grace is not suddenly opening one's life to what is transcendent or to something that has been awaiting entrance within—it is acknowledgment of what is already present and at work in one's life. In the words of theologian John B. Cobb Jr.: "Human beings do not first exist in separation from God's presence within them. They exist by virtue of their inclusion of the divine within them."[41] It's beautifully expressed in the anonymous text of a classic Christian hymn:

> *I sought the Lord, and afterward I knew*
> *he moved my soul to seek him, seeking me;*
> *it was not I that found, O Savior true;*
> *no, I was found of thee.*
>
> *I find, I walk, I love, but oh, the whole*
> *of love is but my answer, Lord, to thee;*
> *for thou wert long beforehand with my soul,*
> *always thou lovest me.*[42]

Paragraph 10's plea to be "vulnerable to divine grace" is an ongoing litany reminding us of God's consistent call to become who we are intended to be—children of God's kingdom of grace.

---

[38]Craddock, F. B. *Luke: Interpretation, a Bible Commentary for Teaching and Preaching* (Louisville, Ky.: John Knox Press, 1990), 182

[39] R. Maurice Boyd, in *A Lover's Quarrel with the World* (Burlington, Ontario, Canada: Welch Publishing Company, 1983), 80.

[40] Lucinda Vardey in *God in All Worlds: An Anthology of Contemporary Spiritual Writing*, edited with introductions by Lucinda Vardey (New York: Vantage Books (Random House), 1995), 385.

[41] John B. Cobb, Jr., *Grace & Responsibility: A Wesleyan Theology for Today* (Nashville: Abingdon, 1995), 40.

[42] Lyrics: Anonymous, circa 1880. This hymn's first publication was apparently in Boston, Massachusetts, in *Holy Songs, Carols and Sacred Ballads*.

Paragraph 10: Questions for Reflection and Discussion

1. **Discernment Exercise**: Find a quiet place. Sit silently for several minutes. Empty your mind of concerns and distracting voices. Acknowledge you are in the presence of the Holy. Read paragraph 10 **several times** aloud or silently. Do so without searching for its meaning or interpretation. Simply read it repeatedly and allow the text to **choose you**. Close the text and sit silently for a short period. What words or phrases begin to surface? With pen and pad write down whatever insights or thoughts come to mind.

2. The mystery of divine love is that it neither increases when we live according to God's will, nor decreases when we live in violation of God's will. Does unmerited love, nevertheless, lay an obligation on us? Can love go unanswered? Discuss the commentator's statement: "God's love is always seeking, but never requiring."

3. The Doctrine and Covenants is replete with references to establish the peaceable kingdom, e.g., "The call is for workers in the cause of Zion" (Doctrine and Covenants, 155:6). Repeatedly we have been admonished to labor for its cause. Ours has not only been a work ethic, it has been a theological work ethic. A works-oriented people see themselves as "working out" their salvation, yet salvation is only possible through God's grace. Discuss the meaning of grace (God's unmerited, everlasting love) in a group.

4. Reflect on a time when pride, fear, or guilt prevented you from drawing close to others and God. How did you come to terms with these feelings of estrangement? How have you been able to help others in like circumstances?

5. Years ago the popular Pogo cartoon character said, "We have met the enemy, and it is us." We are prone to getting in our own way. What does being "vulnerable to divine grace" require of the church as a community? What does it require of you personally?

Reading: "Rehearsal's Resurrection"

Some doors should remain closed, God.

Yes, I know, this goes against trust, openness,
    and faith that even the darkest memories
    can be pierced by light and reconciliation.

So be it.

But, the mantra that one must confront the dark to defeat it
    makes little sense when the enemy's disempowered
    and no longer permitted rehearsal's resurrection.

Get over it. Close the door.

Nail it shut. Move on.

Isn't that what forgiveness is about?

There's something sad about enjoying poor spiritual health
    —opening the door over and over again to past misfortunes.

Free me from the litany that showing my scars
    in the mirror of self-acknowledgment redeems me.

I am more than that. And so are you, God.

The horizon that calls is not behind me.

Past tragedies and sin have had their day.

And, yes, they've helped in their own strange way
    to pave my walk today.

So, let them be. Let them rest.

New possibilities await, straight ahead.

New doors—some good, some not so good.

No hesitation, no looking over my shoulder.
    Grant me courage to open them.

Prayer of Contrition

Tell us how it is done, God.

How do you love us when we are so often unlovable?

How do you continually reach out to us,

     yearning for a response that is forever lethargic or vacant?

What wonder! What patience!

Help us receive your grace.

Deep down we know why we fail to do so.

It's a matter of head and heart.

Sweep away the leftovers of sin

     that will not let us go.

Make us vulnerable once again.

Birth in us the innocence of childhood,

     which celebrates joy at no cost.

For only then will we discover anew

     the blessings of your gospel.
Amen.

Reading: "Delicate Balance"

Days continue to fold in on each other.

Not a blurring of time, just its natural flow.

Natural flow? My, how that phrase slips off

    my tongue so cavalierly.

I must not escape the wonder of it all.

This fortuitous concourse of atoms that makes up me

    and all the other me's.

The mathematical odds boggle the greatest minds.

Billions of stars, black holes, asteroids,

    comets, planets, and things unnamed

    swimming and spinning in space,

    light years apart and as close as next door.

And here I sit on this blue orb that rotates at just the right angle,

    the precise orbit, not too close and not too far

    from a fiery star—that grants me warmth and life.

This tiny round spec whirling for eons on gravity's string,

    a hair's degree from fire and ice.

A delicate balance. A mixture of stardust and hope.

A remarkable blending of gasses, wind, water, soil, and sea

    bubbling up the soup of life.

And perhaps, most astonishing of all—"consciousness"

    —to be awake and aware (in my better moments)

    of this splendid mystery.

And more than that—much more—

    to think that I may address the One

    who puts it all in play.

Quirks, and quarks, and Deity.

Such a delicate balance

    —to reach out, teetering at the edge of thought itself,

    to touch the finger of God

        and sense a smiling face.

We Are Yours

Tune from Sing a New Song #15

1a. You've yearned for us and carried us
Throughout our days, throughout our nights.

1b. Your gracious deeds have favored us
And shown the way with mercy's light.

Refrain

Come, Holy Spirit, pour your grace upon us—
We are yours, and yours we'll always be.

2a. Your steadfast love with grace abounds,
Its length and width no measure's found

2b. Uncaused, unbound it sets us free
From shame and guilt without one plea.

Refrain

Come, Holy Spirit, pour your grace upon us—
We are yours, and yours we'll always be.

3. May our praise be living words
Wrapped in deeds, by love conferred.

Refrain

Come, Holy Spirit, pour your grace upon us—
We are yours, and yours we'll always be.

Notes

Paragraph 11:
What Matters Most

11 a. God is calling for a prophetic community to emerge, drawn from the nations of the world, that is characterized by uncommon devotion to the compassion and peace of God revealed in Jesus Christ. Through divine grace and wisdom, this faith community has been given abundant gifts, resources, and opportunities to equip it to become such a people. Chief among these is the power of community in Christ expressed locally in distinctive fashions while upholding a unity of vision, foundational beliefs, and mission throughout the world.

b. There are many issues that could easily consume the time and energy of the church. However, the challenge before a prophetic people is to discern and pursue what matters most for the journey ahead.

The phrase "to emerge" in the first sentence of paragraph 11 does not presuppose that a "prophetic community" has yet to exist or that such a community will suddenly and mystically materialize in response to God's call. We, like others before us, have responded to the prophetic call to establish Zion—God's kingdom on earth. To emerge is "to come forward"—"to become known." Paragraph 11 is a call to action—reminding us that we have been "given abundant gifts, resources, and opportunities" to be God's prophetic people—a people who can embody God's shalom.

At a time when my word has clearly sent you forth to witness of my gospel, there are many who still are temporizing, looking for further confirming signs of the truth of those instructions which have already been given.—Doctrine and Covenants 155:6

Said another way, "*Zionic conditions are no further away nor any closer than [our] spiritual condition justifies*" (Doctrine and Covenants 140:5c). Sometimes, belief in God's omnipotence gets in our way, fostering the delusion that the peaceable kingdom is *God's work* with a little part-time help from us. Has the kingdom been postponed because *we* have placed it beyond reach? Is there a note of divine frustration in this paragraph? Is God simply "calling" or is God *yearning, praying,* and *pleading* for a prophetic community to emerge?

A prophetic community seeks to embody truth. Its people lay bare what it means to live life anew infused by the highest moral and ethical values. Theirs is a love that calls for sacrifice—not as virtue—but as a willing price to pay on behalf of those who know not love. Their stewardship is a joyful response to God's unbounded generosity. A prophetic community does not wait for the kingdom of God on earth—its people live it, to the best of their ability, in the *here and now*—as step by step they discern its fuller expression.

As mentioned earlier, such a community will not be *one-size fits all*. It is to be "drawn from" a rainbow of diverse cultures, each contributing uniquely to its realization. We have long abandoned the concept that Zion is rooted in one place and populated by one people. It is to live here, there, anywhere, and everywhere people demonstrate an "uncommon devotion to the compassion and peace revealed in Christ Jesus" in signal communities that "uphold a unity of vision, foundational beliefs, and mission throughout the world."

> b. There are many issues that could easily consume the time and energy of the church. However, the challenge before a prophetic people is to discern and pursue what matters most for the journey ahead.

Happiness consists in finding out precisely what the "one thing necessary" may be, in our lives, and in gladly relinquishing all the rest. For then, by a divine paradox, we find that everything else is given us together with the one thing we needed.
—Thomas Merton, *No Man Is an Island*[43]

Paragraph 11b cautions us to not be distracted by the many issues that constantly vie for our attention. The verb "consume" in the first sentence is particularly apt. Not only are we consumed, at times, with peripheral concerns—they consume us.

With the possible exception of cultures in developing nations, today's fast-paced societies suffer from *over-scheduling*. Many North American families do not know what it is to sit down and have a meal together and have succumbed to "hi-tech" at the expense of "high-touch." The *breadwinner* has become the *castle builder*, measuring his or her success by the height of a living-room ceiling, the number of bathrooms and bedrooms in a home, and the make of the car in the driveway. Mistakenly, they believe their loved ones need more *things* when what they need is more of *them*.

What is true for society is true for the church—it, too, can find its "time and energy" consumed by matters that detract from its central call and mission. Some congregations find themselves stretched too thin by trying to be all things to all people. Barely able to enlist sufficient volunteers for a growing list of ministry programs, they suffer burnout and lack of focus. Congregations need to discover "what matters most"—the *Big Yes!* that is *their* unique focus of ministry. When a congregation clearly discerns its *Big Yes!,* peripheral programs and activities can be laid aside. The beauty of a *Big Yes!* is that it gives you the power to say no to competing values that drain effectiveness and dilute mission.

The counsel to discern what matters most, however, is not just addressed to congregational programming, but to a much deeper concern. Specificity of what may be a particular emphasis for the church may fluctuate as circumstances dictate, but we must be wary that such emphasis not cloud our vision. At times we have put undue weight on splitting theological hairs, finding ourselves divided over issues that sap the energies and spiritual life of the church.

The spirit of unity must prevail if my church is to survive these perilous times and continue as a viable force in the world....Put aside petty differences and join together as never before that all may labor together according to the gifts with which I have endowed you.
—Doctrine and Covenants 150:12a–b, excerpts

Your concerns have been my concerns and your tears my tears as divisions, separations, reductions in participation, and limited resources have jeopardized the vigor of my body, the church....But know, dear Saints, the voices of doubt and the spirit of discouragement are strong and will continue to diminish your spiritual energy if you do not strive always to overcome them with a new outpouring of love and support for one another.
—Doctrine and Covenants, 158:9b–10

Carl Jung said, "We count for something only because of the essential we embody, and if we do not embody that, life is wasted." What is "the essential" we embody? This question is succinctly answered in Section 163's paragraph 3b, "Above all else, strive to be faithful to Christ's vision of the peaceable Kingdom of God on earth." Paragraph 11's challenge to "discern and pursue what matters most" is not, then, a puzzle to be solved or a divine mystery to be unwrapped. It is a matter of keeping our eyes on the big picture and not on passing snapshots. To use Paul's words to the Philippian saints, our primary concern is to "Press on toward the goal for the prize of the heavenly call of God in Christ Jesus" (Philippians 3:14). Eugene Peterson's contemporary interpretation in *The Message* puts it this way:

> **I'm not saying that I have this all together, that I have it made. But I am well on my way, reaching out for Christ, who has so wondrously reached out for me. Friends, don't get me wrong: By no means do I count myself an expert in all of this, but I've got my eye on the goal, where God is beckoning us onward—to Jesus. I'm off and running, and I'm not turning back. So let's keep focused on that goal, those of us who want everything God has for us. If any of you have something else in mind, something less than total commitment, God will clear your blurred vision— you'll see it yet! Now that we're on the right track, let's stay on it.**[44]

Ministerial program emphases may indeed express themselves in different ways and be redefined for clarification to meet the needs of a changing church and society, but the central call to pursue God's peaceable kingdom will not change—and this is what matters most!

---

43 Lucinda Vardey in *God in All Worlds: An Anthology of Contemporary Spiritual Writing,* ed. with introductions by Lucinda Vardey (New York: Vantage Books [Random House], 1995), 68.

44 Peterson, E. H. *The Message: The Bible in Contemporary Language* (Philippians 3:12–16) (Colorado Springs: NavPress, 2003).

Paragraph 11: Questions for Reflection and Discussion

1. **Discernment Exercise:** Find a quiet place. Sit silently for several minutes. Empty your mind of concerns and distracting voices. Acknowledge you are in the presence of the Holy. Read paragraph 11 several times aloud or silently. Do so without searching for its meaning or interpretation. Simply read it repeatedly and allow the text to **choose you**. Close the text and sit silently for a short period. What words or phrases begin to surface? With pen and pad write down whatever insights or thoughts come to mind.

2. Passion, enthusiasm, and total commitment often make the difference in achieving what may appear to be an impossible task. Reflect on a time when "uncommon devotion" saw you through a difficult or trying experience.

3. The cause of Zion will always be beyond our reach if we rely solely on our own efforts. A prophetic community "drawn from the nations of the world" is a multicultural (and multi-theological) journey. What foundational principles, relationship skills, and character strengths would be found in such a people?

4. Paragraph 11 states that we presently have "abundant gifts, resources, and opportunities" to become God's prophetic community. What, then, is lacking—what is preventing its fuller expression? Chief among these gifts is the "power of community." Power can be used or abused. In what ways can your congregation exercise its power of community to bless those within the scope of its influence?

5. What "unity of vision" does the Community of Christ uphold? Discuss your understanding of our "foundational beliefs and mission throughout the world."

6. In recent years, there has been considerable emphasis on the gift of discernment. As mentioned in the preface of this study, the 2007 World Conference profiled and modeled a "discernment group" process. If you participated in this activity at Conference, discuss your experience. Would this process be helpful in your congregation? Discuss ways individuals can exercise the gift of discernment.

7. In your opinion, what are some issues that have unduly consumed the time and energy of the church?

8. We are a people who honor our past and, with God, co-create the future. Ours is a unique calling to be a prophetic people. Discuss what you believe "matters most" for the journey ahead.

Reading: "No Longer Postponed"

Paradise postponed.

The dream. The yearning.

The great hope that hope is not enough,

 that somehow—above, beneath, beyond, within—

 the universe will speak at last its sacred name

 in every fragile soul, and love will have its way.

"One reality!"—"Zion"—"The Peaceable Kingdom"

Here and now, not there and then!

No longer postponed.

No longer trapped in godly talk and honeyed phrases

 filled with meaning, bereft of life.

Paradise—freed from feathered angel wings,

 dreamland ecstasies, and wispy mansions in the sky.

The dream. The yearning.

Enslaved no more by onion-skin promises

 held fast by literal Holy Writ.

May new horizons stretch our hopes

 and let us strain to reach them.

A glimpse, a grasp, a fleeting tug

 to pull them home at last.

No longer cast beyond the pale

God's dream alive postponed no more,

Set free beyond our yearning.

Prayer of Petition:
"When Will God Be God?"

When will God be God—when will love be love?

When will Monday be Sunday?

When will each day be Sabbath

    and each meal Eucharist?

When will fists become handshakes,

    hate become love, war become peace?

When will differences bless, not burden?

When will hope find its way and every child be fed

    and every face be honored?

Are these but daydreams, God,

    or are we fast asleep, content to live the nightmare

    of disunity—our dance of self-indulgence?

Let us awaken, God, to your promises.

You have given us abundant gifts and opportunities

    to be your people.

Bless us, then, again, with another portion of your divine grace

    —so that your community of peace

    may indeed emerge in its entire splendor.

Perhaps not complete—not perfect or pristine

    —but growing and glowing with each step we take.

In your servant's words, Lord:

    "Let us write the vision, and make it plain

    upon the tablets of our lives,

    so that even a runner may read it."

Amen.

Share the Peace of Jesus Christ

7.7.7.7.D

Tunes: EASTER HYMN (*Hymns of the Saints #277*)
ABERYSTWYTH (*Worship and Rejoice #333*)

Share the peace of Jesus Christ. Learn to love as God loves you.

Love uncaused and freely given Births God's gift of peace in you.

Give your all, don't hesitate, Melt the walls that separate,

Live a life that demonstrates How to love as God loves you.

Share the peace of Jesus Christ. Love the world as God loves you.

Love that blesses all of life—Whirling planets, old and new.

Move from hope, make real God's dream. Mend the earth, its soul redeem.

Grant it peace, its life esteem. Love the world as God loves you.

Share the peace of Jesus Christ. Let its spirit breathe in you—

Resurrecting buried dreams, Tattered lives and hopes renew.

Be its voice, its hands, its feet. Bring redemption and release.

Share the peace of Jesus Christ—Let its spirit live in you.

Share the peace of Jesus Christ With the ones you hold most dear.

Take more time to laugh and play, Hear their hopes, calm their fears.

Be their guardian, guide, and stay. Demonstrate your love each day.

Share the peace of Jesus Christ With the ones you hold most dear.

Share the peace of Jesus Christ. New horizons beckon you.

Let the Spirit guide each step—Let its grace enliven you.

Risk with God uncharted seas—Let the Spirit set you free.

Share the peace of Jesus Christ. New horizons beckon you.

Concluding Reflections

Thank God for poetry! Not its rhythm, meter, or rhyme,
    not even its strained beauty.
No, celebrate its ambiguity
    —its highs and lows stretching for the sublime.
Its faltering phrases unequal to what it seeks to say
    in language divine: the pulse of the heart,
    the dreams of the mind, the wordless cries of the soul.

Poetry not prose
    —no matter-of-factness, no recipes or formulas
    to make Mystery mute.
Poetry, in all its artful forms, is faith's bright window.
Brushstrokes, canvas, wood, and stone.
Symphonies, cacophonies, notes on a page,
    never quite blue enough, true enough,
    wanting, taunting, yearning for more.
A clear note sounded, a rough edge rounded.
A marriage of meanings when words newly wed
    suddenly say what can never be said:
    the telling of God that remains untold.
A dab here, a dab there—just a hint,
    a splash of serendipity sprinkled on canvas,
    an unsurpassed aria,
    a wispy word or two wrapped in metaphor,
    where mind, heart, and spirit play.

Faith measured is faith restrained.
Set it free! Let it ring out in fanciful verse,
    in a singer's song, an artist's sketch,
    a blush of color, a liturgical dance.
Thank God for poetry—good, bad, wanting and waiting,
    stretching and straining,
    never content, never indifferent
    —its soiled song unwilling to be contained.

        —D. A. Belrose

In a keynote address at "Call to Renewal," in Washington, D.C., Bill Moyers declared that Christianity had lost its voice:

> Over the past few years…Christianity lost its voice. The religious right drowned everyone else out. And they hijacked Jesus. The very Jesus who stood in Nazareth and proclaimed, "The Lord has anointed me to preach the good news to the poor." The very Jesus who told 5,000 hungry people that all of you will be fed, not just some of you. The very Jesus who challenged the religious orthodoxy of the day by feeding the hungry on the Sabbath, who offered kindness to the prostitute and hospitality to the outcast, who said the kingdom of heaven belongs to little children, raised the status of women, and treated even the taxpayer like a child of God. The very Jesus who drove the money changers from the temple. This Jesus has been hijacked and turned into a guardian of privilege instead of a champion of the dispossessed.[45]

Section 163 is a clear and compelling call to hear Christianity's voice beyond the walls of our sanctuaries. It is a call to not only hear Christianity's voice, but to embody its counsel "through redemptive relationships in sacred community." Its commission must ring loudly in our ears and spill out freely in acts that heal the bruised and brokenhearted, bring justice to the oppressed, mend severed relationships, and renew purpose to life.

The gospel upholds the inestimable worth of all people. The ground is level at the foot of the cross and none stands outside the grace of its shadow. Section 163 challenges us to find the face of Christ in those of different color and different persuasions—to hear Christ's voice in those who think differently and live differently—to embrace those whose understanding of life is both less than and greater than our own, and whose image of the Divine cries to be seen and set free.

Section 163 is a call to action. The language throughout the document pulsates with challenging imperatives: "You will become"…"Do not be afraid"… "Generously share"…"Create pathways"…"Strive to be faithful"…"Courageously challenge"…"Pursue peace"… "Be especially alert"…"Open your ears"…"Accelerate the work"…"Break free of the shackles"…"Pursue what matters most"…(and perhaps, its overarching theme and plea) "Be vulnerable to divine grace."

As important as these statements are, reducing the impact of Section 163 to a list of phrases robs the section of its poetic power. In the preface to this study, I offered some brief reflections regarding the Divine-human experience of revelation, emphasizing the challenge of capturing such an experience in words. In a sense, religion relies on poetry, not prose. Any theology that defaults exclusively to prose is diminished. Whenever we distill faith into definitive lists of do's and don'ts—whenever our

tired definitions domesticate the mystery of the Divine— wonder no longer claims us; we claim *it* and cut it down to size. The power of metaphorical language is its ability to couch within it more than facts or creedal declarations but something of the ethereal—that which escapes the discursive language of literalism. "What poets do," says Sallie McFague, "is take our literal words, our dead metaphors and by combining them in new ways, make them capable of expressing a new insight…by framing the ordinary in an extraordinary context."[46] Poetic speech is daring, liberating, unaccommodating, uncontained.

The Introduction to Walter Brueggemann's *Finally Comes the Poet: Daring Speech for Proclamation*, is titled "Poetry in a Prose-Flattened Word." Brueggemann writes:

> Reduced speech leads to reduced lives…To address the issue of truth greatly reduced requires us to be poets that speak against a prose world. The terms of that phrase are readily misunderstood. By prose I refer to a world that is organized in settled formulae, so that even pastoral prayers and love letters sound like memos. By poetry, I do not mean rhyme, rhythm, or meter, but language that moves like Bob Gibson's fast ball, that jumps at the right moment, that breaks open old worlds with surprise, abrasion, and pace. Poetic speech is the only proclamation worth doing in a situation of reductionism….It is, rather, the ready, steady, surprising proposal that the real world in which God invites us to live is not the one made available by the rulers of this age.[47]

Into this "prose-flattened world," the preacher/ prophet/poet speaks what is new and what is old so that, in Brueggemann's words, "in this moment of drama the players render the play as a surprise to permit a fresh hearing, a second opinion…It is not only truth disclosed, but it is life disclosed. Life unclosed, life made open…That long-known truth is now greatly enhanced in riches, texture, availability, demand."[48]

Similarly, a cursory review of the foregoing lists of Section 163's challenging imperatives might conclude that these are not, in and of themselves, either novel or new. Indeed, their reiteration is apparent as noted by their inclusion in early sections of the Doctrine and Covenants. Section 163, however, is much more than a rehearsal of ethical mandates; it is more than the sum of its parts. Its message, powerfully and poetically *framed*

[45] Bill Moyers in a keynote address: Call to Renewal, Washington, D.C., May 24, 2004 (see *www.sojo.net/index.cfm?action=magazine.article&issue=soj0408&article=040810x*).

[46] Sallie McFague, *Speaking in Parables* (Philadelphia: Fortress Press, 1975), 50–57.

[47] Walter Brueggemann, *Finally Comes the Poet: Daring Speech For Proclamation* (Minneapolis: Augsburg Fortress Press, 1989) 3.

[48] Ibid., 9, 10.

in the extraordinary context of inspired counsel, reinforces claims of the gospel we frequently ignore and expands our understanding of these principles with new insights that challenge us to move forward on the path of discipleship.

Let me conclude by saying that, in essence, divine revelation is *prayer*—it is God's prayer to us. God has no hands but our hands—no feet but our feet. The raising of hands authorizing a document's inclusion in the Doctrine and Covenants is a blessing to the church, but it is the canonization of its counsel in our hearts, attitudes, and behavior that God passionately desires.

In summary, Section 163 is God's prayer for us to go deeper and soar higher—to plunge the depths and scale the heights of what it means to be a prophetic people dedicated to peace, justice, reconciliation, and healing of the Spirit. Step by step we are beginning to discern what it means to be a peace church—to inculcate into the fabric of who we presently are as a Community of Christ what that name and identity prompts us to discover. It is not enough to be called "Community of Christ." We are called *to become* Christ's community—a people of joy, hope, love, and peace.

Proclaim the Peace of Christ

8.6.8.6.8.6

Tunes: BROTHER JAMES' AIR (*Hymns of the Saints #350*)
DIADEM (*HS #70*)
MORNING SONG (*HS #457*)

It's not enough to sing God's praise And bow our heads in prayer.

It's not enough to preach God's word When wanting souls despair.

Proclaim the peace of Jesus Christ—Make bold his presence here!

It's not enough to kneel in prayer And share in wine and bread.

It's not enough to give our tithes When children go unfed.

Proclaim the peace of Jesus Christ—Become his living bread!

It's not enough to speak of faith With creeds and words extreme.

The time has come to demonstrate A faith that lives God's dream.

Proclaim the peace of Jesus Christ—Each loving deed redeems.

It's not enough to hear God's plea And answer, "Yes, send me!"

It's not enough to sing of peace When life lacks liberty.

Proclaim the peace of Jesus Christ—And set creation free!

It's not enough to praise in song The beauty of the earth—

Creation sings that life is one And nature shares our worth.

Proclaim the peace of Jesus Christ And heal God's wounded earth.

Notes

Notes

Notes